"These books will make super resources for Sunday school classes, for thoughtful church leaders, and indeed for all Christians who want to take their faith, and its ecumenical history, seriously."

CARL R. TRUEMAN, Paul Woolley Professor of Church History,
Westminster Theological Seminary, PA

"Faithful wisdom through the centuries needs to be explored for our own engagement with Scripture today. It takes a gifted scholar to survey these sources well, and a gifted teacher to communicate them to the person in the pew. Justin Holcomb is that sort of scholar-communicator."

MICHAEL HORTON, J. G. Machen Professor of Systematic Theology and
Apologetics, Westminster Seminary, CA; author, *The Christian Faith*

"I welcome the Know series as an important companion in our lifelong quest to know God better."

CAROLYN CUSTIS JAMES, author, *When Life and Beliefs Collide*

"The Know series gives local leaders and churches short, succinct, accurate, theologically informed, and relevant sketches of big topics in theology. Pastors and professors will discover they are unable to keep students from these volumes."

SCOT MCKNIGHT, author, *King Jesus Gospel*

"Jesus promised that the Spirit would lead the church into truth. That means that history matters. These concise books from Justin Holcomb are invitations into that history, to see how the Spirit led the church to articulate the orthodox Christian faith and how that scriptural imagination helped them discern errors and wrong turns. We need this wisdom more than ever in our postmodern moment."

JAMES K. A. SMITH, Gary and Henrietta Byker Chair in Applied Reformed
Theology and Worldview, Calvin College; author, *Letters to a Young Calvinist*
and *Desiring the Kingdom*

"I applaud the Know series in its effort to equip the saints; I encourage pastors and laypeople alike to diligently read these books."

rience Economy

T0084295

Books in the Know Series

Know the Creeds and Councils
Know the Heretics

KNOW
THE
CREEDS AND
COUNCILS

JUSTIN S. HOLCOMB

ZONDERVAN

Know the Creeds and Councils
Copyright © 2014 by Justin Holcomb

This title is also available as a Zondervan ebook.

Requests for information should be addressed to:

Zondervan, 3900 *Sparks Drive SE, Grand Rapids, Michigan 49546*

Library of Congress Cataloging-in-Publication Data

Holcomb, Justin S.
    Know the creeds and councils / Justin S. Holcomb.
        pages cm. — (Know series)
    Includes bibliographical references.
    ISBN 978-0-310-51509-8 (softcover)
    1. Creeds, Ecumenical. 2. Councils and synods, Ecumenical. I. Title.
BT990.H65 2014
    238 — dc23   2013047052

Cover design: Gearbox
Interior composition: Greg Johnson/Textbook Perfect

First printing April 2014 / Printed in the United States of America

CONTENTS

FOREWORD

Why try to understand the councils? We learn something important from them: how the teachings of the prophets and apostles were consensually received by comparing Scripture to Scripture to grasp the meaning of the whole narrative of the history of salvation.

These conciliar decisions have been tested again and again, and have continued to be confirmed by the consent of believers. They reassure us that we can trust the understanding of God's revelation in Scripture that has been held to be true by the whole worldwide church throughout changing cultures of all times and places. These conciliar decisions have been hammered out by intense examination of Scripture when nonconsensual opinions have been asserted. We learn from them those teachings that the ancient Christian consensus has confirmed as true apostolic teaching.

In *Know the Creeds and Councils*, Justin Holcomb accurately summarizes key points of the most crucial, contested issues of scriptural understanding, drawing readers today closer to the truth of classic Christianity.

—THOMAS C. ODEN

ACKNOWLEDGMENTS

First of all, a special thanks to Jeffrey Haines for his superb research assistance and editing. Much gratitude for those who also assisted with research: Jordan Buckley, James Gordon, Jonathan Arnold, Tim McConnell, and Michael Stell.

I would like to thank Donald Prudlo for his suggestions on the chapters on the Council of Trent and the Second Vatican Council.

At Zondervan, I would like to thank my editor, Madison Trammel, who supported the book and series marvelously.

INTRODUCTION

What Are Creeds, Confessions, Catechisms, and Councils?

> Tradition is the fruit of the Spirit's teaching activity from the ages as God's people have sought understanding of Scripture. It is not infallible, but neither is it negligible, and we impoverish ourselves if we disregard it.
>
> — J. I. Packer, "Upholding the Unity of Scripture Today"

Obviously, Christianity did not begin when we were born. Nor did our generation invent Christian thought. We live two thousand years removed from the time of our founder, and — for better or for worse — we are the recipients of a long line of Christians' insights, mistakes, and ways of speaking about God and the Christian faith. Today's Christianity is directly affected by what earlier Christians chose to do and to believe.

The fact that Christianity developed — that the sixteenth century, for instance, looked very different from the third, and that both looked very different from the twenty-first — can sometimes lead us to wonder what the essential core of Christianity is. As a result, some people decide to ignore history altogether and try to reconstruct "real Christianity" with nothing more than a Bible. But this approach misses a great deal. Christians of the past were no less concerned with being faithful to God than we are, and they sought to fit together all that Scripture has to say about the mysteries of Christianity — the incarnation, the Trinity, predestination, and more — with all the intellectual power of their times. To ignore these insights is to attempt to reinvent the wheel, and to risk reinventing it badly.

The main difficulty is untangling the language of the church of the past, particularly for those of us who do not have time or energy to devote to historical studies. The goal of this book is to guide readers past that difficulty and to provide an overview of the main historical developments in Christian thought. It is not intended to be a comprehensive guide to *all* creeds, councils, confessions, and catechisms; that would take nothing less than an encyclopedia. However, I hope that after reading this book you will come away with a deeper and better understanding of how the church has wrestled with what continue to be the most important questions about Christian belief.

The chapters are brief and to the point. For each creed, confession, catechism, or council, I present historical background, a short summary of the content, and thoughts on contemporary relevance. At the end of each chapter are discussion questions and recommended reading for further study.

Before we examine the history itself, it will be important to learn the four major terms that you will encounter in this book. Each one represents a tool that the church has used to speak about God clearly and faithfully, to guide its members closer to God, and sometimes to distinguish authentic Christianity from the innovations, heresies, and false teachings that the New Testament warns of. While their purposes differ, all try to communicate complex theological ideas to people who don't have sophisticated theological backgrounds (in some cases, to people who are illiterate). The four terms are "creeds," "confessions," "catechisms," and "councils."

Creeds

> I believe in God,
> The Father Almighty
> Maker of Heaven and Earth
> Of all that is seen and unseen ...
>
> — Opening lines of the Nicene Creed, AD 325

The English word "creed" comes from the Latin word *credo*, which means "I believe." Church historian J. N. D. Kelly says that a creed is "a fixed formula summarizing the essential articles of the Christian religion and enjoying the sanction of ecclesiastical [church] authority."[1] More simply, the creeds set forth the basic beliefs of the church that have been handed down from earliest times, what the New Testament calls "the faith that was once for all entrusted to God's holy people" (Jude 3). When teachers throughout history called parts of this faith into question (usually the parts that were taken for granted or were less well-defined), the early church reaffirmed the essentials in a way that honored the traditional teaching.

The earliest creeds are arguably to be found in Scripture itself. In the Old Testament, what is known as the Shema ("Hear, O Israel: the LORD our God, the LORD is one," Deut. 6:4) is a creedlike statement. While there are no official, full-blown creeds in the New Testament, scholar Ralph Martin has suggested that the beginnings of creeds are already present in the New Testament and were developed by early Christians to defend against subtle pagan influences and to establish key beliefs.[2] Many scholars believe that Paul recites an early creed in his letter to the Corinthians when he summarizes the facts that he taught as "of first importance": "that Christ died for our sins according to the Scriptures, that he was buried, that he was raised on the third day according to the Scriptures, and that he appeared [to the apostles and many others]" (1 Cor. 15:3–7). Furthermore, in the church's acts of baptism, Eucharist, and worship, certain prayers and early creedlike statements of belief were developed, such as "Jesus is

Lord" (1 Cor. 12:3) and the Trinitarian baptismal formula of Matthew 28:19: "in the name of the Father and of the Son and of the Holy Spirit." While there is no formal creed in the pages of Scripture, the idea of a central, basic teaching of Christianity certainly is.

After the age of the apostles, the early church possessed what is known as "the rule of faith" or "the tradition," which theologian Bruce Demarest describes as "brief summaries of essential Christian truths."[3] Early church fathers such as Irenaeus, Clement of Alexandria, Tertullian, and Hippolytus all assume this "rule of faith," an unwritten set of beliefs that had been passed down from the apostles and taught to Christian converts. In the second century, Irenaeus described the rule of faith in this way: "One God, the Creator of heaven and earth, and all things therein, by means of Christ Jesus, the Son of God; who, because of His surpassing love towards His creation, condescended to be born of the virgin, He Himself uniting man through Himself to God, and having suffered under Pontius Pilate, and rising again, and having been received up in splendor, shall come in glory, the Savior of those who are saved, and the Judge of those who are judged, and sending into eternal fire those who transform the truth, and despise His Father and His advent."[4]

Irenaeus's rule of faith sounds quite similar to later formal creeds and contains the essence of the gospel. As the early Christian community dealt with new heretical movements, the rule of faith gave birth to more precise statements of the essentials of the faith, such as the Apostles' Creed and the Nicene Creed.[5]

How Were Creeds Used?

In individualist cultures, we pick and choose what religion we like. More than that, we sometimes combine parts of different denominations or religions to make something entirely new — whatever works for us personally. For the early Christians, however, creeds were meant to be used by groups — not just a summary of what everyone in the room agrees upon but a promise made and kept as a group.

Creeds were initially used in baptism, during which the baptismal candidate recited a formula or responded to questions, thereby publicly confessing belief in Jesus Christ. As time passed, however, the creeds also were used to teach new converts the basic elements of the Christian faith. Since the creeds were relatively short summaries of Christian doctrine, they were easy to learn. The creeds were also used in church liturgies (the set of actions and rituals in a worship service that illustrate Christian beliefs and mysteries), uniting the congregation in common confession. Far from being a device of the ivory tower, creeds were the way that ordinary tradesmen and farmers could learn about and pledge their lives to the God of the Bible.

Nowadays, we have a largely literate population and an ample supply of Bibles, and so it's easy to wonder whether creeds are necessary. Some may even think that the creeds stand in opposition to (or at least in tension with) the authority of Holy Scripture. However, as theologian John Webster says, "We may think of the creed as an aspect of the church's exegetical fellowship, of learning alongside the saints and doctors and martyrs how to give ear to the gospel."[6] Creeds aren't dogmas that are imposed on Scripture but are themselves drawn from the Bible and provide a touchstone to the faith for Christians of all times and places.

Confessions

Although the light of nature, and the works of creation and providence do so far manifest the goodness, wisdom, and power of God, as to leave men unexcusable; yet are they not sufficient to give that knowledge of God, and of His will, which is necessary unto salvation. Therefore it pleased the Lord, at sundry times, and in divers manners, to reveal Himself, and to declare that His will unto His Church; and afterwards for the better preserving and propagating of the truth, and for the more sure establishment and comfort of the Church against the corruption of the flesh, and the malice of Satan and of the world, to commit the same wholly unto writing; which makes the Holy Scripture to be most necessary; those former ways of God's revealing His will unto His people being now ceased.

— Opening lines of the Westminster Confession on the purpose of Scripture, AD 1646

What about confessions? In contrast to creeds, which are basic statements of belief, confessions represent more detailed inquiry into the things of God. The great writer C. S. Lewis gave the following illustration to show the value of having confessions as well as creeds: "I hope no reader will suppose that 'mere' Christianity is here put forward as an alternative to the [confessions] of the existing communions — as if a man could adopt it in preference to Congregationalism or Greek Orthodoxy or anything else. It is more like a hall out of which doors open into several rooms. If I can bring anyone into that hall [creeds], I have done what I attempted. But it is in the rooms [confessions], not the hall, that there are fires and chairs and meals."[7]

As Lewis's illustration suggests, the creeds are the boundaries of the faith that separate orthodoxy from heresy, while the confessions color in the picture, tying theology to everyday life in all sorts of ways. Because creeds are bare-bones structures (the outlines of the sketch), it makes sense that the earliest statements of the church are creeds, while later statements of particular denominations are confessions. Creeds distinguish orthodoxy from heresy (or Christian faith from non-Christian faith). Confessions distinguish denominational distinctives (or one type of Christian faith from another type of Christian faith).

Christian confessions often define a particular group's belief on secondary issues such as infant baptism, the end times, predestination, the Lord's Supper, and the order of salvation. As a rule, Christian confessions addressed the immediate needs and concerns of those who wrote them. (That is, while the creeds strove to preserve "the faith delivered for all time," confessions tried to apply the faith to the here and now.) Because confessions often arose out of theological debate, the issues emphasized in any particular confession may say more about cross-denominational arguments than anything else; hence, although those issues may still be relevant today, they may not be of the same importance as they were long ago.

Some Prominent Confessions

There are, broadly speaking, two different kinds of confessions. The first is meant to distinguish one denomination from another. Examples of this type of confession include the following:

- The Thirty-nine Articles (Anglican, 1563)
- The Formula of Concord (Lutheran, 1577)
- The Arminian Confession of 1621 (Arminian, 1621)
- The Westminster Confession (Presbyterian, 1646)
- The Dordrecht Confession (Anabaptist, 1632)
- The Augsburg Confession (Lutheran, 1530)
- The Scots Confession (Church of Scotland, 1560)
- The Belgic Confession (Reformed, 1561)
- The First and Second Helvetic Confessions (Lutheran, 1536 and 1562)
- The Twenty-five Articles of Religion (Methodist, 1784)
- The Confessions of Trent (Roman Catholic, 1545–63)
- Vatican II (Catholic, 1962–65)

The majority of these confessions arose during the Reformation. As various sects of Reformation Protestantism were coming into existence, they needed to put forth coherent teachings that distinguished their groups from other denominations.

However, because these confessions could not possibly foresee issues that would arise as later churches tried to live faithfully in contemporary culture, a second type of confession came into existence. This type of confession — illustrated by the Chicago Statement on Biblical Inerrancy and the Lausanne Covenant — puts forth a specific church's (or group of churches') response to a specific theological issue that is of pressing importance for the contemporary church. This second type of confession is typically supplementary; it is not a complete statement of a specific church's beliefs and doctrines but is instead a collaboration among different churches to address a significant issue. (In the previous two examples, one is a response to biblical criticism and the other to the changing face of world evangelism.)

Use of Confessions

While confessions have not been as relevant to worship services as creeds have (it's rare to find a congregation reciting the Twenty-five Articles of Religion on a given Sunday), they still play an important role in the life of the church. First, confessional statements form the basis of catechisms, which are used to introduce new believers and children to the basic teachings of the church. Second, confessions help a denomination to maintain doctrinal unity by providing a standard to which the teaching of individual congregations should adhere. This standard helps maintain denominational integrity and preserves the ideals of the group against cultural trends or the doctrinal innovations of an individual leader.

Some may worry that church confessions are archaic, that they undermine the overarching unity of the body of Christ, or that they nitpick over relatively insignificant issues of doctrine. While there may be some legitimacy to these critiques, it is important to keep in mind that confessions are meant to be worshipful responses to a truly gracious God. It isn't enough for believers to stop at a basic knowledge of God, as Lewis so shrewdly noted, even though the basics tie together all the variations within orthodox Christianity. God has given us a lot of information about himself that a creed does not cover; it is within confessions that churches interpret that information and show believers how it can help them know God better. Seen in this light, the confessions of the church take on a new beauty, a beauty that finds its origin in the God of the gospel and in the salvation he offers to his people.

Catechisms

Q. What is your only comfort in life and in death?

A. That I am not my own but belong — body and soul, in life and in death — to my faithful Savior, Jesus Christ.

He has fully paid for all my sins with his precious blood, and has set me free from the tyranny of the devil. He also watches over me in such a way that not a hair can fall from my head without the will of my Father in heaven; in fact, all things must work together for my salvation.

Because I belong to him, Christ, by his Holy Spirit, assures me of eternal life and makes me wholeheartedly willing and ready from now on to live for him.

— Opening question of the Heidelberg Catechism, AD 1563

A catechism is a book or document giving a brief summary of the basic principles of Christianity in Q&A form. Catechisms represent the practical, "on-the-ground" application of the main teaching agreed upon at church councils and expressed through creeds and confessions. The word "catechism" comes from the Greek word *katechein*, which means "to teach" or "to instruct." Catechisms are basic outlines of the teachings of the Christian faith, set forth in a way that those unfamiliar with doctrine can easily understand.

Catechisms have been around since the early church, which was quite devoted to instructing new believers in the Christian faith. Since conversion was a radical change from one way of life to another, Cyril of Jerusalem made the following description of the process: "Let me compare the catechizing to a building. Unless we methodically bind and joint the whole structure together, we shall have leaks and dry rot, and all our previous exertions will be wasted."[8] The process of catechesis was also alive and well in the Middle Ages: Aquinas wrote a catechism that was basically an extended explanation of the Apostles' Creed, one of the earliest summaries of the Christian faith.

However, the era most commonly associated with catechisms is the Reformation, "the Golden Age of catechisms."[9] In fact, one scholar calls the catechism "the heart of the Reformation."[10] Martin Luther, who wrote both a small and a large catechism, put the burden of catechizing on parents, not the church: "If everything cannot be covered at once, let one point be taken up today, and tomorrow another [point]. If parents and guardians will not take the trouble to do this, either themselves or through others, there never will be a catechism."[11]

John Calvin also thought the process of catechesis was incredibly important.[12] Calvin was concerned that his congregation be instructed in the basic teachings of the gospel so that they could fight off the attacks of Satan. Indeed, Calvin thought that the success of the church was largely dependent on how it catechized its youth, which is why he wrote and revised a catechism for his church. In addition to Calvin and Luther, John Owen and Richard Baxter also wrote a variety of catechisms appropriate for various age groups.

Early Christian catechesis focused on immersion in God's Word, basic instruction in doctrine, and ethical and moral guidelines.[13] Catechisms in the Reformation were similar, but they implemented a question and answer format that had become popular in the Middle Ages. In this style, the person writing the catechism was able to anticipate questions and objections from those reading the document. Because of the widespread illiteracy during the period of the Reformation, catechesis often took place in face-to-face discussion. This is why "Luther intended his catechism to target primarily pastors, but also parents, and other 'opinion makers' who would in turn share the teachings of the catechism orally with children and illiterate members of the household."[14]

Uses of Catechisms

Catechisms are designed to work on multiple levels for learners' best retention. As Nordling notes, "Luther intended that the Small Catechism would come to constitute the Christian's internal 'computer operating system' (for example, DOS, Windows, Mac OS), which would become fixed in the immediate stores of memory, and thereby become the foundation for approaching God and all things spiritual."[15] For instance, the basic content of Luther's smaller catechism was to be memorized first, and the Scripture references supporting the basic answers were to be memorized at a later date. In this way, the catechism provided both an intimate acquaintance with the Bible as well as a guidebook for reading and understanding the Bible.

It is important to remember that catechisms are not meant to be an end in themselves. They are to lead to belief, practice, and love for God. As such, the counterparts to catechisms are confessions. Put most simply, catechisms teach in order that we may confess and believe. John Webster says that "through [a creed or confession] the church affirms its allegiance to God, repudiates the falsehood by which the church is threatened, and assembles around the judgment and consolation of the gospel."[16] However, the activities that Webster describes take place not only in church buildings but also in homes, offices, schools, and private conversations, so catechisms are tools to bring confessional beliefs into our daily lives.

Examples of Catechisms

Perhaps the most common catechisms today are those which are products of the Protestant Reformation: Reformed Westminster Catechism (shorter and larger), the Lutheran Small Catechism in the Book of Concord, and my favorite — the Heidelberg Catechism. While the content of these catechisms is a bit advanced, the introduction to the Westminster Shorter Catechism is an excellent tool for children. The Catechism for Young Children is used in many denominations as an introduction. Also, author Chris Schlecht has written a children's catechism, which explains the basics of the Reformed faith. The Catechism of the Church of Geneva for children may also be a good choice for parents who want to learn how to teach their children about the faith.

Church Councils

Canon 1
We have judged it right that the canons of the Holy Fathers made in every synod even until now, should remain in force.

— Council of Chalcedon, AD 451

Many of the creeds, confessions, and catechisms of the church were decided upon at large church meetings called councils. Councils brought together leaders from all over the known world to hammer out issues, such as responses to heretical teachings, that were too difficult for individual pastors or bishops to handle alone. There are seven ecumenical councils that every branch of the church[17] recognizes today, whether Orthodox, Catholic, or Protestant, and there have been fourteen additional Catholic councils.[18]

The first recorded instance of a church council is found in the New Testament. The Jerusalem Council is the name that was given to the meeting of church leaders of Antioch (with Paul and Barnabas) and of Jerusalem in which the large growth in the number of Gentile converts in the early church was discussed (Acts 15:2–29).[19] The issue being addressed was a practical one concerning how Jewish and Gentile Christians would relate to one another on a daily basis. Gentile Christians were to abstain from certain activities that would be barriers for relationships with Jewish Christians, such as eating food offered to idols (see Rom. 14:1–23; 1 Cor. 8:1–13). As a result of that council, it was also agreed that Gentile Christians did not have to become Jewish or observe Jewish practices to worship God, even though God had chosen the Jews as his special people.

Because the council allowed these changes to be put into place in all the represented churches (rather than on a case-by-case basis), it prevented individual leaders from requiring churches they led to conform to their own ideas about the Jewish question.

Like the Jerusalem Council, later church councils were called to address not only a disagreement over a theological issue but also the practical ramifications of that issue. For instance, in the Council of Nicaea, the question being asked was, "How can we worship one God (the Father) and also worship Jesus Christ?" Though this was a practical question about worship, it couldn't be disconnected from the more abstract theological issue of how Jesus Christ is related to his Father. The council affirmed that both Jesus and the Father are members of a single being, God.

So are the councils' decisions authoritative? It is instructive to notice that in 1 Corinthians when Paul is asked about whether Christians should eat food offered to idols (in 1 Cor. 8:1 – 13), he appeals not to the decision of the Jerusalem Council but instead to the revelation he had received from Jesus Christ. This shows that Paul saw the Jerusalem Council as in some sense authoritative but not ultimately so. His appeal was to God's revelation as the arbiter of truth, not to a human decision at a council.

Uses of Councils

Councils bring together Christians from all over the world — not just the best and brightest thinkers, the flashiest preachers, or the most fervent activists but a cross section of informed Christian leaders. Ideally, the diversity that a council brings — both in the origins of the attendees and in their viewpoints — ensures that all viewpoints are fairly represented. Having asked the Spirit to guide their decisions, these Christians then try to work out a solution to the questions at hand that is best in line with Scripture.

Yet the councils didn't always follow this ideal. They were sometimes marked by politics and dissension, even the use of force. The way that key questions about God were decided may make us wonder whether the lines that councils drew between orthodoxy and heresy are worth keeping or whether they are simply part of the struggles of a bygone age. Does it matter whether we believe that God is a trinity or that Jesus is both God and man?

In retrospect, the decisions of the councils seem to have been best. (They say hindsight is 20/20.) Contrary to the everyday perception that the church devised a dogma and then imposed it on the unwilling masses (the "extremists" on the "moderates," as medieval Muslim scholar Ibn Taymiyya phrased it), the story of the councils is one in which the complexity and ambiguity of Scripture is defended time after time against oversimplifications that would have lost something crucial to the faith. If the proceedings of the councils were not always the best examples of witness to Christ, they nevertheless held the church together against a wrongful decision. Think of it as comparable to the Union and the Confederates in the American Civil War. That war still scars our national memory, but it was necessary to prevent our country from going in an unfortunate direction. In the same way, there is much to be grateful for in the councils.

Know the Creeds and Councils

This book aims to provide an accessible overview of the main creeds, confessions, catechisms, and councils of Christian history. It is an introduction to some of the most important theological declarations in the Christian tradition. It is not intended to be a comprehensive guide to *all* creeds, councils, and confessions; that would take nothing less than an encyclopedia. However, I hope that after reading this book, you will come away with a deeper and better understanding of how the church has wrestled with major doctrinal questions and has emerged stronger as Jesus continues to build his church.

Know the Creeds and Councils is not an academic book or only for "educated lay readers." It is designed to be read by individuals or used in a group setting. My hope is that this book will complement more thorough treatments such as Jaroslav Pelikan's *Credo: Historical and Theological Guide to Creeds and Confessions of Faith in the Christian Tradition*, which is a nearly seven-hundred-page book filled with top-notch historical scholarship on the creeds and confessions.

The chapters are brief and to the point. For each creed, confession, catechism, or council, I present its historical background, its content, and its contemporary relevance. Because some readers will prefer to look at just a few specific issues, I have tried to strike a balance between letting each chapter stand alone and building the narrative as things unfolded historically. Discussion questions and recommendations for further reading are included at the end of each chapter.

Further Reading

Bickersteth, Edward Henry. *The Trinity: The Classical Study of Biblical Trinitarianism*. Grand Rapids, MI: Kregel, 2000.

Bright, William. *The Canons of the First Four General Councils of Nicaea, Constantinople, Ephesus, and Chalcedon*. Oxford: Clarendon, 1892.

Bromiley, Geoffrey. *Historical Theology: An Introduction*. Grand Rapids, MI: Eerdmans, 1978.

Brown, Harold O. J. *Heresies: Heresies and Orthodoxy in the History of the Church*. Peabody, MA: Hendrickson, 2003.

Chadwick, Henry. *The Early Church*. Rev. ed. New York: Penguin, 1993.

Crisp, Oliver. *Divinity and Humanity: The Incarnation Reconsidered*. Current Issues in Theology. Cambridge: Cambridge Univ. Press, 2007.

Davis, Leo Donald. *The First Seven Ecumenical Councils (325–787): Their History and Theology*. Collegeville, MN: Liturgical Press, 1983.

Frend, W. H. C. *The Rise of Christianity*. Philadelphia: Fortress, 1984.

Kelly, J. N. D. *Early Christian Doctrines*. Rev. ed. San Francisco: HarperCollins, 1978.

Kelly, Joseph F. *The Ecumenical Councils of the Catholic Church: A History.* Collegeville, MN: Liturgical Press, 2009.

McGrath, Alistair E. *Historical Theology: An Introduction to the History of Christian Thought.* Malden, MA: Blackwell, 1998.

Olson, Roger E. *The Story of Christian Theology: Twenty Centuries of Tradition and Reform.* Downers Grove, IL: InterVarsity Academic, 1999.

Pelikan, Jaroslav. *The Emergence of the Catholic Tradition (100–600).* Vol. 1 of *The Christian Tradition: A History of the Development of Doctrine.* Chicago: Univ. of Chicago Press, 1971.

Schaff, Philip. *History of the Christian Church.* Vol. 2. 1858. Peabody, MA: Hendrickson, 2006.

Schaff, Philip, and Henry Wace, eds. *Ante-Nicene Fathers.* Vol. 1. Reprint. Peabody, MA: Hendrickson, 1995.

——. *Ante-Nicene Fathers.* Vol. 3. Reprint. Peabody, MA: Hendrickson, 1995.

——. *Nicene and Post-Nicene Fathers: First Series.* Vol. 5. Reprint. Peabody, MA: Hendrickson, 1995.

——. *Nicene and Post-Nicene Fathers: Second Series.* Vol. 4. Translated by Cardinal Newman. Reprint. Peabody, MA: Hendrickson, 1995.

CHAPTER 1

APOSTLES' CREED

ca. 140

Historical Background

The Apostles' Creed is the oldest creed of the church, and its influence can be seen in many of the subsequent creeds in church history. The Apostles' Creed[1] was so named because of a tradition that emerged in the sixth century that each of the apostles contributed one of the creed's twelve articles, or statements of belief.[2] This story, although ancient, is almost certainly a legend: the Apostles' Creed is not a direct production of the apostles themselves. Rather, the justification for continuing to call this formulation the Apostles' Creed is that it preserves the "rule of faith" that was transmitted from the apostles. It should be understood as a summary of apostolic teaching.[3]

The creed is an early witness to the apostolic teaching, and not an attempt to attribute a later document to the apostolic era. This can be seen from its development from the so-called Old Roman Creed that was used during baptisms, which can be dated from the middle of the second century (about AD 140) in Greek and in Latin around AD 390. The Old Roman Creed featured the main tenets of the Apostles' Creed, with a few additions that are explained in the next section. The present form of the Apostles' Creed, which is both longer and more recent, was probably not compiled until the middle of the fifth century.[4]

During the Middle Ages, it became commonplace to recite the Apostles' Creed throughout the day in Western monasteries, and this practice was retained in the Book of Common Prayer in the Church of England after the Reformation, where it is still recited during morning and evening prayer. Many churches still recite it during baptisms as a summary of the faith into which Christians are baptized.

Church historian Philip Schaff notes that "as the Lord's Prayer is the Prayer of prayers, the Decalogue [10 Commandments] the Law of laws, so the Apostles' Creed is the Creed of Creeds."[5] Perhaps more than any other profession of faith, the Apostles' Creed has expressed the essentials of Christianity in a way that Christians of all stripes can rally around. Early theologians, like Irenaeus, Tertullian, and Origen, affirmed various parts of the creed. John Calvin devoted an entire chapter to the Apostles' Creed in the first edition of his *Institutes of the Christian Religion* (1536), and Karl Barth presented his entire system of doctrine through the framework of the creed in *Dogmatics in Outline*. Today, the Apostles' Creed has been at the heart of much of the movement toward Christian unity of the twentieth century. To give only two examples, in 1920 the Lambeth Conference of the Anglican Communion appealed to it as the basis of unity among all Christian churches, and in 1927 at the World Conference on Faith and Order that met at Lausanne, Western and Eastern Christians recited the Apostles' Creed in unison during the opening session.[6] The Apostles' Creed has been and continues to be of great importance for Christians worldwide.

Content

The Apostles' Creed is brief enough that its entire content can be reproduced here:

I believe in God, the Father Almighty, the Maker of heaven and earth, and in Jesus Christ, His only Son, our Lord: Who was conceived by the Holy Ghost, born of the virgin Mary, suffered under Pontius Pilate, was crucified, died, and buried; He descended into hell. The third day He arose again from the dead; He ascended into heaven, and [sits] on the right hand of God the Father Almighty; from thence he shall come to judge the quick and the dead. I believe in the Holy Ghost; the holy catholic church; the communion of saints; the forgiveness of sins; the resurrection of the body; and the life everlasting. Amen.

If you could go only by this creed (the earliest collection of "essentials"), what would you say that Christianity is? As we will see in the following chapter, on the Council of Nicaea, several key doctrines are not made explicit here: the relationship of Christ to God, and the identity of the Holy Spirit are the most obvious ones that modern Christians would miss. However, it is encouraging and surprising how many of the doctrines that we hold today appear here. There's the incarnation ("Christ ... was conceived by the Holy Ghost"), and the story of the Gospels ("suffered ... was crucified, died, and buried ... He arose again from the dead; He ascended into heaven"). There isn't yet an explicit doctrine of the Trinity, but the creed wants the reader to know that God is tied to the names of Father, Son, and Holy Ghost, and that Christ is said to still be alive and preparing for his role as cosmic judge. God's forgiveness of sins and promise of physical resurrection are also present, and it is reasonable to assume that these are connected to the snapshot of the gospel story that accompanies the description of Christ. In short, knowing nothing else about Christianity, you could find out who God is, the story of what happened to Jesus of Nazareth, and what will happen next.

However, the creed also contains phrases such as "descended into hell" and "the holy catholic church" that may make modern Protestants pause. These are also essential elements of the Christian faith (now just as much as then), but since both of these phrases took on specific meanings during the Middle Ages, it is important to understand how ancient Christians would have seen them.

For those who grew up in a Roman Catholic context, the expression "he descended into hell" may be familiar because it is associated with the doctrine of the "harrowing of hell." In Catholic theology, the idea is that after Christ's death on the cross, his spirit descended into sheol (the word in Hebrew for the "underworld," where the dead reside) in order to preach the gospel to the patriarchs, the Old Testament saints, and potentially to other "virtuous" pagans who lived before the revelation of Jesus Christ.[7]

Much of this discussion is not based on the Bible. The New Testament itself emphasizes the consequences of Christ's death and resurrection from the dead, in which he triumphs over sin, death, and the devil, rather than what Christ did between death and resurrection.[8] Initially the language of "descent into hell" was borrowed from the Old Testament; it simply meant that Jesus died or passed to sheol (the pit or grave) just as any other person did.[9]

Dying was the final stage of Christ's humiliation, a necessary passage before his triumph in the resurrection. Second-century theologian Tertullian wrote that "Christ our God, Who because He was man died according to the same Scriptures, satisfied this law also by undergoing the form of human death in the underworld, and did not ascend aloft to heaven until He had gone down to the regions beneath the earth."[10] The Latin translations of the creed themselves do not agree on how to phrase this doctrine: some have that he descended *ad inferna* ("into hell"), and others *ad inferos* ("to the dead"). The latter reflects more closely, it seems, the intention of the creed.[11] A number of contemporary translations reflect this understanding by changing the language of the creed to "he descended to the dead."

The second potentially troublesome expression in the creed is "the holy catholic church." Because only the Roman Catholic Church retains "Catholic" in its name, some Protestants might hesitate to confess that they believe in a catholic church. However, the word "catholic" is actually a way to refer to the whole church of Jesus Christ, deriving from two Greek words, *kata* and *holos*, which together mean "according to the whole." The term is usually translated in Protestant churches as "universal," but this does not quite do justice to its richness. "Catholic" means that the church exists in every nation where the gospel has spread. Second-century church father Ignatius of Antioch wrote that "wherever Jesus Christ is, there is the Catholic Church,"[12] and fourth-century father Cyril of Jerusalem wrote that the church is catholic not only "because it is spread throughout the world" but also "because it teaches completely and without defect all the doctrines which ought to come to the knowledge of men."[13] Wherever the whole apostolic gospel is visibly maintained, that is where the "catholic church" is.

In general, the creed remains as accessible to believers today as it was two thousand years ago. Despite the updates (see the section on historical background), the Apostles' Creed is as good a tool as any for finding out what early Christians believed, and to seeing how similar it is to what we believe now.

Relevance

Much of the genius of the Apostles' Creed is in how it shows the supernatural significance of historical events. In a secular age, God the Father, the ascended Christ, and the Holy Spirit seem much less certain than the things that we can see and experience every day. The message that God has forgiven sin because of Christ's sacrifice seems distant from the reality of a crucified religious leader. In the early church, it was important to ground religious belief in the historical life and death of Jesus of Nazareth — hence the gospel snapshot in the creed — against the elaborate myths of their rivals, the Gnostics, who were interested in Jesus as a figure for their spiritual allegories. In our day, we have the opposite challenge: how do we keep up our religious beliefs when the mundane realities of our daily lives make it hard to grasp that God interacts with our world?

The Apostles' Creed answers both challenges. It denies that the Christian story is merely myth, but it also affirms that we have a glimpse into the supernatural world through it. It goes on to show the outworking of the historical Jesus and the supernatural world in our daily lives. The communion of saints and the forgiveness of sins are ways in which we can relate to and experience God, because of Christ, and through the Holy Spirit, in our everyday, mundane lives, proving that the supernatural still breaks through into the world. And it ends by reminding us that, just as Jesus' time on an ordinary earth ended with his ascension into a very unordinary glory, so too will our everyday experience of the Holy Spirit end with our own resurrection and exaltation. C. S. Lewis wrote, "It is a serious thing to live in a society of possible gods and goddesses, to remember that the dullest most uninteresting person you talk to may one day be a creature which, if you saw it now, you would be strongly tempted to worship, or else a horror and a corruption such as you now meet, if at all, only in a nightmare ... it is immortals whom we joke with, work with, marry, snub, and exploit — immortal horrors or everlasting splendors."[14]

The Apostles' Creed reminds us of this reality, and the reason for our hope, in clear, simple terms.

Discussion Questions

1. Based on the Apostles' Creed, what would you say the early Christians believed? Do you see anything that's missing?
2. As the next chapters will show, the Apostles' Creed was still vague about certain theological issues. Which areas do you think might be problematic?
3. How could you, your family, or your church group use the Apostles' Creed as a devotional tool?

Further Reading

Barth, Karl. *Dogmatics in Outline*. New York: Harper Perennial, 1959.

González, Justo L. *The Apostles' Creed for Today*. Louisville: Westminster John Knox, 2007.

Horton, Michael. *We Believe: Recovering the Essentials of the Apostles' Creed*. Nashville: Thomas Nelson, 1998.

Johnson, Luke Timothy. *The Creed: What Christians Believe and Why It Matters*. New York: Doubleday, 2003.

McGrath, Alister. *"I Believe": Exploring the Apostles' Creed*. Downers Grove, IL: InterVarsity, 1998.

Packer, J. I. *Affirming the Apostles' Creed*. Wheaton, IL: Crossway, 2008.

CHAPTER 2

COUNCIL OF NICAEA AND THE NICENE CREED

325

Historical Background

What we call the Nicene Creed is actually the product of two ecumenical councils — one in Nicaea (present-day Iznik, Turkey) in AD 325, and one in Constantinople (now Istanbul) in AD 381 — and a century of debate over the nature of the relationship between the Father, the Son, and the Holy Spirit. The Nicene Creed is perhaps the most famous and influential creed in the history of the church, because it settled the question of how Christians can worship one God and also claim that this God is three persons. It was the first creed to obtain universal authority in the church, and it improved the language of the Apostles' Creed by including more specific statements about the divinity of Christ and the Holy Spirit.

In AD 324, Constantine reunited the Roman Empire under a single throne. Constantine was himself a recent convert to

Christianity, having (temporarily) ended all persecution by decree in AD 313 after he claimed that he won a battle by calling out to the Christian God. It was Constantine who convened the first ecumenical, fully representative, universally recognized council of the Christian church. While it is common today to overemphasize Constantine's role and authority in influencing the shape of Christianity as we know it (he did not declare that Jesus is God or decide the books of the New Testament by any stretch of the imagination), there is no doubt that this was one of the critical turning points in Christianity.[1]

The council was summoned to resolve a problem that had sprung up seven years earlier and had left the Christian church fiercely divided. In Alexandria in AD 318, a presbyter (elder) named Arius began publicly proclaiming his theory that Jesus was not God at all, only a celestial servant of the true Most High God, who alone was almighty, transcendent, the creator and first cause of all things. After all, Jesus was prone to emotion (as opposed to the Father, who was always in control of his emotions), grew and learned (as opposed to the Father, who never changed), and died (as opposed to the Father, who is immortal). Only the Father could be considered uncreated and "timelessly self-subsistent."[2]

Arius thought that his interpretation had good footing in the theology of the great teacher Origen of the prior century. Origen had said that the Father was due glory and reverence as God himself (*autotheos*) that was not due to the Son.[3] Arius's bishop, Alexander, disagreed, pointing out that Origen also said "Father" is an eternal attribute of God. This means two things: first, since it's not possible to be a father without also having offspring, the fact that God is eternally a father means that he eternally has a son.[4] Furthermore, Alexander pointed out, God is perfect and not subject to change, so how could God change from not being a father to being a father? In attempting to preserve the dignity of the Father, Arius was tampering with some of the crucial distinctions that separate God from humanity.

But it was not ultimately so much a debate about Origen as a debate about Scripture. At places, Jesus seems to suggest that he is subordinate to the Father (for example, John 14:28). At the same time, Scripture is equally clear that Jesus is and claimed to be both divine and equal with the Father as God (John 1:1; 5:16–18; 10:30; 14:6–14). The question is how we can worship Jesus and worship the Father (who we know is different from Jesus) and still claim to be monotheists who worship one true God? (Many people today, such as Muslims, have particular trouble with this idea.) After years of fierce division that stretched from clergy to the common people, the ecumenical council was summoned to resolve the issue once and for all.

Content

The final form of the Nicene Creed reads as follows (note that the footnotes mark later changes to the creed):

I believe in one God, the Father Almighty, Maker of heaven and earth, and of all things visible and invisible.

And in one Lord Jesus Christ, the only-begotten Son of God, begotten of the Father before all worlds; God of God, Light of Light, very God of very God; begotten, not made, being of one substance with the Father, by whom all things were made. Who, for us men and for our salvation,[5] came down from heaven, and was incarnate by the Holy Spirit of the virgin Mary, and was made man; and was crucified also for us under Pontius Pilate; He suffered and was buried; and the third day He rose again, according to the Scriptures; and ascended into heaven, and sits on the right hand of the Father; and He shall come again, with glory, to judge the quick and the dead; whose kingdom shall have no end.

And I believe in the Holy Ghost,[6] the Lord and Giver of Life; who proceeds from the Father and the Son;[7] who with the Father and the Son together is worshipped and glorified; who spoke by the prophets. And I believe in one holy catholic and apostolic Church. I acknowledge one baptism for the remission of sins; and I look for the resurrection of the dead, and the life of the world to come. Amen.

The creed follows basically the same structure as the Apostles' Creed — that is, it mentions all three members of the Trinity in a similar order and retains the snapshot of the gospel story when it describes Jesus. It expands the description of the life and work of Christ, explicitly stating that his mission was "for us and for our salvation." Like all of the ecumenical creeds, the Nicene Creed does not set forth any specific theory or view of atonement — the way of understanding what Jesus accomplished on the cross. Still, in its final form, the creed tells us that Christ's mission for our salvation included coming down out of heaven and taking on flesh from the Virgin Mary (the incarnation), carrying that flesh in suffering through life and into death on the cross. The creed declares that he was crucified by Pontius Pilate, "for us." (*Huper humon* here in the Greek can carry a lot of meanings. "For us," "because of us," or even "in place of us" are all possible readings and can give us some insight into what the common faith of Christians is.) Somehow or another, Christ died for us to take our place of suffering and set us free to receive salvation. The creed deliberately draws on tradition to show that the ideas put forward here are not an innovation to the "faith delivered once for all."

The main difference between this creed and the Apostles' Creed, however, is a new, expanded section on the relationship between Jesus and the Father, since the chief concern of the council was to defend the true divinity of the Son against Arius. The creed asserts this by professing the "Lord Jesus Christ" to be the "Son of God," "begotten of the Father," "only-begotten." These are biblical assertions (Mark 1:1 and 1 John 4:15 call Jesus the Son of God; Acts 13:33 and Heb. 5:5 speak of him as begotten of the Father; John 1:14 and 3:18 both use the Greek word *monogenous*, which means "only-begotten"). Jesus, they claim, is God: "God from God." If you need an analogy, the next phrase serves. It's like light. How can you separate light from light? You can't. (This was a traditional example in early Christian writings, usually concerning the ray of the sun and the sun itself.) Neither can the Father and the Son be separated. Then it repeats for emphasis that Jesus is "very God of very God"; he is not made or created or a product of the true God. Jesus *is* the true God.

Athanasius was at the council as a deacon in the service of Alexander. He later recounted that up to this point, the Arians were still on board. In fact, they were winking and snickering at one another, as if to say, "This is fine. We can still get around this."[8] Something more had to be added to defend orthodoxy, even if it could not be stated using only biblical terminology. Something was needed that would settle once and for all that the divinity of Jesus is the divinity of the Father, one and the same. It was agreed to make it clear that this Jesus is forever and eternally "of one substance with the Father." By insisting that the Son is "of one substance" with the Father, the Arian view was rejected and the council affirmed that the Father is not "more God" than the Son. God is God, in trinity.

Because the council was primarily interested in discussing Jesus, the original form of the creed did not have much to say about the Holy Spirit. (The creed was updated after the first Council of Constantinople to reflect the deity of the Holy Spirit.) However, there is a great deal that is said implicitly about his divinity. It is best to read the Nicene Creed as three articles. It begins, "We believe in …" and then suspends two subparagraphs: " … and in one Lord Jesus Christ," " … and in the Holy Spirit." It is Trinitarian in form. Understanding it this way, we see all that follows as part of the third article of the creed — the Holy Spirit's article. To the Holy Spirit, and to his activity, belong the holy catholic and apostolic church, its teaching, its confession, its sacraments, and its ultimate new birth into the resurrection of everlasting life. Put simply, the Holy Spirit is the one who leads the church in its worship and its confession of the triune God.

Relevance

Because it is recited in many churches every Sunday, the Nicene Creed is familiar to many Christians. Like the Apostles' Creed, it encapsulates the entire good news of the gospel into a short and rich summary. It describes the triune God, who turns toward humanity in the person of Jesus, the God-man who suffered, died, rose again, and ascended. Additionally, the creed goes on to express our future hope, the purpose of living the Christian life.

However, it is the Nicene Creed, not the Apostles' Creed, that describes the minimum of Christian belief. By sad experience, the leaders of the church found that there were areas in the "rule of faith" that left too much open to personal interpretation. The fact that Jesus and the Holy Spirit are just as much God as the Father is a nonnegotiable part of Christianity. It is not that Christians are expected to have a perfectly precise Trinitarian theology to be considered orthodox, but since questions about the relationship between Jesus and God the Father are inevitable, they needed to be answered well. The Nicene Creed encapsulates what Scripture says about that relationship and acknowledges the mystery of it.

If Christianity had agreed with Arius that Jesus could be a lesser god — if it had failed to defend monotheism, if it had fallen into the trench of professing three unrelated deities — it may have dissolved into the religion of Rome and its pantheons of false gods. If the early Christians had lost their nerve and conceded the "lesser divinity" of Jesus, whatever that might mean, then the work of God in Christ for our salvation would have been rendered meaningless. No mere man, nor half god, could possibly intervene to save fallen and sinful humanity, let alone restore all of creation. Only the Creator can enter creation to fix its brokenness and redeem its original, latent purpose. Athanasius explored this truth in *On the Incarnation*, defending the claim that the Father and the Son share one common substance (*homoousios*). Only the Creator can recreate. Only the Maker can remake. Only God can save us from our sins.

Because the Father and the Son are one substance, we can also be assured that we actually know God in Jesus Christ. After all, "The Son is the radiance of God's glory and the exact representation of his being" (Heb. 1:3), and so when we look on Jesus, we look on God. Without confidence that Jesus is God, united in substance with the Father, we could not be sure that Jesus can speak for God, forgive sins for God, declare righteousness for God, or do anything to make us children of the Father.

Discussion Questions

1. Why is it critical that Jesus Christ is actually, fully, and essentially God — "of the same essence" as the Father?
2. What does "of the same essence" mean? Even if the Trinity is beyond our comprehension, how would you translate that into everyday language?
3. What images or metaphors do you use to understand the Trinity? Can you see their shortcomings?
4. Why can't a half god save humanity?

Further Reading

Ayres, Lewis. *Nicaea and Its Legacy*. Oxford: Oxford Univ. Press, 2004.
Behr, John. *The Nicene Faith*. 2 volumes. Crestwood, NY: St. Vladimir's Seminary Press, 2004.
Torrance, T. F. *The Trinitarian Faith*. Edinburgh: T&T Clark, 1988.
Williams, Rowan. *Arius: Heresy and Tradition*. Rev. ed. Grand Rapids, MI: Eerdmans, 2001.

CHAPTER 3

COUNCILS OF EPHESUS

431, 449, 475

Historical Background

Like the city of Constantinople, Ephesus was home to several church councils: the First Council of Ephesus (431), the Second Council of Ephesus (449), and the Third Council of Ephesus (475). However, only the First Council of Ephesus is recognized as an ecumenical council of the church.

The period between 428, when the following controversy began, and Chalcedon in 451 is one of the most important periods of christological discussion in the history of the church. ("Christology" is the study of the doctrine of the nature of Christ. Some samples of christological questions are found in the following sentences.) The orthodox position had always been that Christ was both God and man, and the Council of Nicaea, in 325, had codified this position: "We believe in one Lord, Jesus Christ, the only Son of God, eternally begotten of the Father, God from God, Light from Light, true God from true God, begotten, not made, of one Being with the Father ... For us and for our salvation he came down from heaven: by the power of the Holy Spirit he became incarnate from the Virgin Mary, and was made man." But it was one thing merely to say that Jesus was both God and man; since he was a historical person, what did that mean? How much God was he, and how much man? Did it mean that he had two minds — a divine and a human one — which seems impossible, or did it mean that the divine part of him overwhelmed the human part, which seems to contradict the idea that he was fully human? All of these questions seem abstract and even irrelevant, but they had and continue to have implications for the way that Christians see the life of Jesus. To take only one scenario, think of how differently his temptation in the desert would be interpreted if he had a divine but not a human mind. Or consider his redemptive sufferings on the cross — what if he were suffering only as an ordinary human being, or conversely only as a human body propelled by a divine control center? Would that change how we look to Christ for inspiration or even salvation?

The Council at Ephesus attempted to resolve a dispute between two answers to these questions, one that emphasized the fact that Christ was fully human and fully divine to the point where it seemed as though he were two persons, and one that emphasized his unity but offered little explanation as to what being both divine and human meant. In the process, the council took a step toward the full-fledged Christology that later emerged at Chalcedon. However, as J. N. D. Kelly notes, "at no phase in the evolution of the Church's theology have the fundamental issues been so mixed up with in the clash of politics and personalities."[1] Because the theology that emerged from Ephesus was so closely tied up with unpleasant political realities, this chapter will examine both the issues discussed at the council and the ways in which the two sides attempted to manipulate its decision.

People and Places

The Council of Ephesus represented the end of a clash between two powerful church officials: the Patriarch of Constantinople, Nestorius, and the Patriarch of Alexandria, Cyril. Their two theological approaches will be discussed below, but their political careers also had an impact on the events of the council.

Nestorius had been recently appointed as Patriarch of Constantinople by the time of the council. Fervent, stubborn, and politically naive, he quickly alienated many of the people in the city. For instance, having assured the emperor, Theodosius II, that the empire would triumph over its enemies once the emperor threw out all heretics, Nestorius proceeded to burn down a chapel belonging to members of the Arian heresy.[2] A great deal of the city also burned as a result of the fire, which earned Nestorius the nickname "Torchie."[3] In another instance, he refused a request by the Roman pope, Celestine, to return another group of heretics who were taking refuge in Constantinople.[4] Nor did he show himself open to listening to different points of view. When he could not answer the questions of some monks during one of his sermons, he invited them to come to his house the following day to discuss the matter further. When the monks arrived, however, they were beaten by Nestorius's guards.[5] In a short time, Nestorius had made an impressive number of enemies, although he had enough friends among the nobility to ensure his continued reign as patriarch.

Cyril, meanwhile, was earning much the same reputation across the sea in Alexandria. His tenure as Patriarch of Alexandria saw the murder of a female pagan philosopher,[6] as well as the breakdown of secular Roman authority in favor of rule by militant monks.[7] Unlike Nestorius, however, he had had twenty-five years of political experience by the time of the council and is generally held to have been a deeper thinker and more profound theologian than his rival.

It was perhaps inevitable that these two men would clash over both politics and theology. Not only did Cyril and Nestorius come from two of the most powerful cities in the world, but these cities also had long opposed each other on christological interpretation. Nestorius's home diocese, the Syrian city of Antioch, favored a historical, literal approach that emphasized the humanity of Jesus, while the Alexandrian school in Egypt was prone to emphasize Jesus' godhood.[8] When battle lines were drawn at the council, the bishops split along largely ethnic lines — Syrians supported Nestorius, while Egyptians, Greeks, and Romans (whom Nestorius had alienated) backed Cyril.

To modern readers, the political background to the council can seem jarring. It is useful to remember that the ancient world operated under different conceptions than ours does. For instance, both Nestorius and Cyril believed that it was vital for the empire to hold the proper ideas about Christ in order for its people to prosper. Both were placed in a situation in which they were expected to forge political connections and wield authority, even authority backed by the use of force. These circumstances might not excuse the actions that they undertook to win the council, but it must be understood that they were not simply power-hungry fanatics. As the following section will show, both patriarchs were deeply concerned with understanding the nature of Christ in a way that was true to Scripture and that would lead others to salvation.

Nestorian Christology

Nestorius developed his Christology in the light of two major heresies that were threatening the Christian world: Arianism and Manichaeanism.[9]

Arianism (discussed in the previous chapter) argued that Christ was not God but only a celestial being that God had used to accomplish his purposes. To support their view, Arian theologians argued that God is impassible, a technical philosophical term that means that God is not controlled by emotions. If God is affected by emotion, it means that something other than God could hold power over God, which then means that God himself is not all-powerful. Orthodox theologians subscribed to the doctrine of impassability as well. Arians, however, took the logic of impassability one step farther. They said that since Jesus was passible, or affected by emotions, he could not be God. Instead, he was a demigod, God and man mixed together.

Manichaeans, on the other hand, took the opposite approach. Convinced that the material world was evil and that Jesus had come not to free us from sin but to free our souls from matter, the Manichaeans argued that Jesus was not a man at all. He was a divine being clad in human form, like a cloak, which he put on or off at will.

Nestorius attempted to form a Christology that would uphold orthodox Christian teachings against these two heresies and others like it. Against the Arians, who mingled the human and divine parts of Jesus, Nestorius held firmly to the belief that Jesus was both fully God and fully man, and that these parts were separate. Thus, Jesus could really suffer for the redemption of humankind in his passible, human part, but remain in control and impassible in his divine part.[10] Against the Manichaeans, who believed that a human Christ would actually be a detriment to salvation, Nestorius tended to emphasize that Jesus was fully human in all points. That Jesus was human in every possible way was crucial to the way that Nestorius conceived of the atonement — in his body, Jesus was a substitute for those who were like himself, so that they would be able to pass through death into the resurrected life: "And since many are brought low by the fear of death, he endured unto death and gave a just compensation for us in that he exchanged for our death the death which came unjustly upon him."[11] If Jesus was somehow not like us, his atonement would be invalid.[12]

Nestorius wanted to reject any sort of suffering in the divine nature of Christ as well as to affirm that the human nature of Christ grew and was tempted. In his mind, the separation of the natures of Christ and the emphasis on Christ's humanity did not mean that Jesus was two separate people or that he was not fully God.[13] Although his opponents often accused him of holding such positions, it is important to understand that Nestorius himself did not believe that he had overstepped any boundaries.

Cyrilline Christology

If Nestorius emphasized the humanity of Jesus as crucial for salvation, Cyril believed that the real importance lay in the divinity of Jesus. What Cyril found most troubling about Nestorius's two-nature theory was that the humanity of Jesus could potentially be so opaque that the divinity of Jesus would not be able to shine through. Cyril argued that if Jesus had two natures, one God and one man, and if to everyone around him he seemed to be like every other man, then he could offer no more salvation than Moses could. Those who worshiped Jesus would worship only the outward, human form,[14] and those who were reshaped in his image would be reshaped to resemble only his human nature.[15] For Cyril, Nestorius's theory threatened the idea of Jesus as the "express image of God" and "God among us."

Furthermore, Cyril thought that Nestorius's theology threatened the unity of Jesus, and ended by making Jesus into two people who were loosely tied together. He was just as concerned as Nestorius with establishing Jesus as a human being rather than as a God who was cloaked in humanity, but he thought that if Christ suffered only in his human form, he would not be an effective high priest.[16] Cyril held that it was through *divine* suffering that Christ mediated the sins of humankind, and so even though the suffering of God on the cross might be a paradox, it is nevertheless a nonnegotiable principle of the faith.

Events at the Council

Nestorius came to the center of theological controversy when, after arriving at Constantinople, he was asked to comment on whether it was fitting to call Jesus' mother Mary Theotokos ("Mother of God"; literally "Bearer of God"). For Nestorius, who wanted to keep the two natures of Christ separate, this was a difficult assertion to make. While he maintained that Mary did indeed give birth to Christ, Nestorius thought it was inappropriate to speak of Mary as being the mother of God when she bore the child Jesus. God is eternal, and any attempt to say that God was born of Mary seemed to Nestorius to be closet Arianism (since Arianism taught that there was a time when the Son of God did not exist). He said that he could affirm *Theotokos* if *Anthropotokos* ("Mother of Man") was added to her title, but he considered *Christotokos* ("Mother of Christ") the most fitting title, for as J. N. D. Kelly notes, "God cannot have a mother, [Nestorius] argued, and no creature could have engendered the Godhead. Mary bore a man, the vehicle of divinity but not God."[17]

In 429, Cyril had heard of Nestorius's dismissal of *Theotokos*, and the two exchanged a series of heated letters. Both men appealed to Pope Celestine, who quickly held a synod in Rome (430) in order to affirm the title *Theotokos* against Nestorius. Cyril informed Nestorius of the ruling and ordered him to cease his teaching and recant his position; he wrote a long letter to Nestorius consisting of twelve anathemas, which were "deliberately provocative."[18] It is likely that Cyril's new statement of anathemas was unfair, as it represented a more extreme version of Nestorius's view than he himself held. Consequently, Theodosius the emperor called a meeting in June of 431 at Ephesus. This meeting, later known as the First Council of Ephesus, was the climax of the conflict between Cyril and Nestorius.

From the beginning, however, the council was slanted in Cyril's favor. Although the council had been slated to take place at Constantinople, the sister of the emperor, Pulcheria, moved it to Ephesus.[19] Pulcheria was a longtime enemy of Nestorius and knew that Ephesus was the site of a thriving shrine to Mary. The locals at Ephesus obviously favored the title of *Theotokos*, and their opinions became a key factor in the debate.

Nestorius thought that Cyril's theology led to a God who was too closely unified — if Jesus were only God, unmediated by a distinctly human part that could absorb the shocks and experiences of the world, then it made sense to say that what was apparently true of Jesus' human part was true of God. In an unfortunate blunder, Nestorius said that he refused to worship a God who was a baby of two or three months old.[20] By this he meant that if Mary were the mother of God, then it was implied that she was the mother of God in all his fullness — an obvious absurdity. The Cyrilline party took this statement as an opportunity to paint Nestorius as a heretic. They accused him of believing that Christ was a man whom God later made divine (also known as the "adoptionist" heresy), a charge that was made more credible by the fact that Nestorius's home city of Antioch had produced a prominent adoptionist not long before named Paul of Samosata. The people of Ephesus either believed the charge of adoptionism or used it as an excuse for their own ill will toward Nestorius, because threats were soon made against bishops friendly to Nestorius, and several abandoned him for Cyril's side.[21]

The council decided against Nestorius. He was stripped of his power and rank and driven into exile, where he tried to rally support against Cyril with his own council, but was unsuccessful. Because Nestorius had several supporters among the nobility of Constantinople, Cyril was also imprisoned for a time. However, he was allowed to return to his office, and for the next two decades, his Christology dominated the theology of the empire.

The Legacy of Ephesus

Sympathizers of Nestorius fled the empire to Mesopotamia and Persia, where they established themselves in the intellectual center of the Persian church, at Nisibis. The Persian church continued to honor Nestorius and eventually separated itself from the West when the Persian Empire began to clash with the eastern Roman Empire. In the next few centuries, Nestorian missionaries planted churches in Iran, India, Central Asia, and up to the coast of China.[22] Some of these communities survive to the present day. Inadvertently, the decision at Ephesus resulted in the expansion of Christianity; without the seemingly harsh ruling of the council, there would have been much less incentive to bring the gospel to those new territories.

Relevance

The political struggles of Ephesus can pose a problem for modern-day believers. Even if denominations might differ on how difficult theological questions are resolved, it seems obvious that they should not be resolved the way that those at Ephesus were — with underhanded political tactics and a refusal to understand the points of the other side. The fact that one of the major councils of the church seems to depend just as much on politics as theology can be disturbing — can we be sure that the church made the right decision? Are the beliefs that we hold today the result of careful interpretation of Scripture, or the machinations of powerful figures? It is helpful to remember that the story of redemption in the Bible relies on people who deliberately did evil things — Samson, Saul, and David are excellent examples. When Jesus came, however, it became apparent that God not only had accounted for human failing but had even made it a part of his plan for the salvation of the world; as Joseph says to his brothers in Genesis 50:20, "You intended to harm me, but God intended it for good to accomplish what is now being done, the saving of many lives." Because God is able to work through human failings as well as in spite of them, Christianity does not need to rely on a whitewashed version of history.

At the same time, we should recognize that Ephesus represents an important development in Christian theology. Despite their personal rivalry, both sides were seriously trying to understand how Christ saves humankind, and the questions that they raised are worth deep consideration. How human was Christ? Did his humanity dilute or mask his divinity? Did his divinity interfere with the effectiveness of his sacrifice? As we have seen, the council came down firmly on the side that promoted the unity of Christ's being, and despite the political wrangling, it did so because it considered Nestorius's Christology as the beginning of a slippery slope that might disconnect Christ from his divinity in all but name. Later, at Chalcedon in 451, the council revisited the issue and refined the decision that it had made at Ephesus in a way that resolved some of Nestorius's concerns, but by taking a decisive stand for Christ's being a single person, the church had moved one step closer to a more articulate Christology that helped believers better understand the work of salvation.

Finally, we can learn to exercise great caution and care when dialoguing with people with whom we disagree. Theologian Kevin Vanhoozer described such virtue as "dialogical virtues," which he defines as "honesty, fairness, and clarity ... [and] in particular humility, the opposite of pride or self-righteousness. The dialogical virtues, first cousin to the intellectual virtues, aim to [create] right communication and right thinking ... And make no mistake, the dialogical virtues that I've just enumerated are ultimately the fruit of the Holy Spirit."[23]

Ephesus reminds us to ask for those virtues from God in all humility.

Discussion Questions

1. Cyril's theology depended heavily on divine suffering. How does divine suffering impact the Christian faith?
2. Nestorius thought that the unity of Christ's person resulted in one of two problems — either Christ became a demigod, or he lost his humanity.
   a. Was he right? Do you see either of these trends today? (For instance, do people tend to think of Christ only as God?)
   b. What is redemptive about Christ's human nature?
3. How would you have ruled as a member of the council? Was emphasizing the unity of Christ really an important issue?

Further Reading

Chadwick, Henry. *The Church in Ancient Society: From Galilee to Gregory the Great.* Oxford: Oxford Univ. Press, 2001.

Clayton, Paul B. *The Christology of Cyrus: Antiochene Christology from the Council of Ephesus (431) to the Council of Chalcedon (451).* Oxford: Oxford Univ. Press, 2007.

Cyril of Alexandria. *Five Tomes against Nestorius.* Oxford: James Parker and Co., 1881.

Fairbairn, Donald. *Grace and Christology in the Early Church.* Oxford: Oxford Univ. Press, 2003.

McGuckin, John. *St. Cyril of Alexandria and the Christological Controversy.* Crestwood, NY: St. Vladimir's Seminary Press, 2004.

Nestorius. *The Bazaar of Heracleides.* Translated by G. R. Driver and Leonard Hodgson. Oxford: Clarendon, 1925.

CHAPTER 4

COUNCIL OF CHALCEDON

451

Historical Background

The Council of Nicaea left unanswered the exact relationship between the man Jesus Christ and the eternal Son of God — the *Logos* of the gospel of John (1:1–4, 14). Based on this passage in John and the hymn in Philippians 2:5–8, the church had for four hundred years confessed the incarnation of the Son of God, but the full ramifications of the incarnation were not yet formally developed. How could Jesus be both human and God? Although the church rejected early attempts by the Gnostics (a collection of hyperspiritual religious groups) to say that Jesus was a helpful spirit who only appeared to be a man, it became much more difficult to think through the implications of what the Scriptures seemed to say — that Jesus was both man and God. Justo Gonzalez said of this theological dilemma, "Both sides were agreed that the divine was immutable and eternal. The question then was, how can the immutable, eternal God be joined to a mutable, historical man?"[1] Nestorius had proposed one idea of how this might work, but the

Council of Ephesus had dismissed it as inadequate in 431 because it made it difficult for believers to treat Jesus as a person in the way that one normally treats a person. The church had not yet articulated a thorough response, and as long as the issue was left open, the possibility of serious error was a real one.

That possibility soon became apparent in Eutyches, the head of a monastery on the outskirts of Constantinople. Eutyches was staunchly anti-Nestorian, but he fell into trouble in the opposite direction. For Eutyches, the emphasis was on the union of the two natures of Christ, to the point that while there were two natures before the union, there was only one nature after the union of the incarnation; this view is called Monophysitism (*physis* is the Greek word for nature). This meant that instead of a union, there was a mixture of the two natures into a new "third nature" that was neither divine nor human. Eutyches agreed with Cyril that there was only one person, but unlike Cyril, he adamantly refused to say that there were still two natures in the person of Jesus Christ.

The Council of Chalcedon — the fourth ecumenical council of the church — dealt specifically with the two natures of Jesus Christ. Just how, the council asked, did God become human? How, in other words, could the church navigate the extremes of Nestorianism, on the one hand, and Eutychianism, on the other? In 451, the church met to settle this question.

The Council of Chalcedon

The council began on October 8, 451, with more than five hundred bishops in attendance, the largest gathering in a church council thus far. Pope Leo sent a group to represent him, and his comprehensive work on Christology, known as the "Tome," played an important role in creating the most significant christological statement of the faith the church had yet produced.

To reaffirm that the council was continuing tradition, the statement developed at Nicaea was read along with the letter from Cyril to Nestorius and the Tome of Leo. The bishops approved both the creed and the theological works as sufficient to solve the problems that had plagued the Eastern churches over the past fifty years. However, the emperor wanted a new creed developed that would not just unite the Antiochenes and the Alexandrians (those who emphasized the humanity of Christ and those who emphasized the divinity) but the whole of the Christian world — East and West.[2] While not all of the bishops agreed that a new creed was needed, a committee was appointed to develop a draft that could be debated and voted upon.

The first draft presented to the council generally pleased everyone, except for the papal representatives. At issue was what to say about the two natures of Christ. The language that was originally drafted was too close to Eutychian or Monophysite language (that one nature overwhelmed the other). Originally it used the simple phrase "out of two natures," and the papal representatives said that this did not do enough to secure the notion of the two natures remaining distinct in the one person of Jesus Christ, the eternal Son of God. Leo's Tome used the phrase "two natures are united without change, and without division, and without confusion in Christ."[3] When the changes were made, the resulting statement of faith shows that "while rejecting the extremes of both Alexandrines and Antiochenes, and particularly the doctrine of Eutyches, it reaffirmed what had been done in the three previous great councils."[4]

The Definition of Chalcedon

The council was clear that the formulation of Chalcedon was not a new creed but an interpretation and elaboration of previous decisions. The Definition of Chalcedon itself is a statement of both simplicity and great depth, aiming to set out a coherent christological position that walked the line between the Nestorian heresy (two persons in Christ) on the one hand and the Eutychean heresy (only one nature in Christ) on the other:

Therefore, following the holy Fathers, we all with one accord teach men to acknowledge one and the same Son, our Lord Jesus Christ, at once complete in Godhead and complete in manhood, truly God and truly man, consisting also of a reasonable soul and body; of one substance [*homoousios*] with the Father as regards his Godhead, and at the same time of one substance with us as regards his manhood; like us in all respects, apart from sin; as regards his Godhead, begotten of the Father before all ages, but yet as regards his manhood begotten, for us men and for our salvation, of Mary the Virgin, the God-bearer [*Theotokos*]; one and the same Christ, Son, Lord, Only-begotten, recognized in two natures, without confusion, without change, without division, without separation; the distinction of natures being in no way annulled by the union, but rather the characteristics of each nature being preserved and coming together to form one person and subsistence [*hypostasis*], not as parted or separated into two persons, but one and the same Son and Only-begotten God the Word, Lord Jesus Christ; even as the prophets from earliest times spoke of him, and our Lord Jesus Christ himself taught us, and the creed of the Fathers has handed down to us.[5]

The definition can be divided into two basic parts. The first part is a restatement of the Nicene Creed, with the addition of the *Theotokos* phrase from Ephesus (431). The second part combines the theology found in the writings of Cyril and Leo. The first part restates the important phrases of the fullness of both Jesus' divinity and his humanity. The phrasing used is that Christ is *homoousios*, or of one substance, with the Father in his divinity and with us in his humanity. This maintained the fullness of the two natures in the incarnation. The council wanted to make it clear that a human nature was not something occupied by Christ, but that Jesus Christ was a man, just like every other man, except without sin. In keeping the *Theotokos* language, they were acknowledging that the union of the two natures in the one person allowed the use of the communication of properties: the impassible God suffers in the human person Jesus Christ, and the human person Jesus Christ is the creator of the universe. The Definition of Chalcedon described Christ's descent as a true incarnation of the *Logos*, the Second Person of the Trinity, while denying that a man was converted into God or that God was converted into a man. There was no confusion or absorption between the divine nature and the human nature of Christ; the two remained distinct. Similarly, the incarnation was not merely a divine indwelling of a human nor a connection between two persons. Instead, Chalcedon asserted that there was a real union between the divine and human natures that existed in one personal life: the life of Jesus of Nazareth, who was the eternal *Logos*.

The second paragraph develops the important christological statements about the person of Christ. Most of these statements were influenced by Cyril and Leo. The statement "without any confusion, change, division or separation" excludes both Eutychian and Nestorian teachings. Against Eutyches, the creed also says that the union does not destroy the difference between the two natures; there is not a third nature created in the union. Each of the two natures retains its properties. Against Nestorius, the definition declares that these two natures are joined into one person. There can be no separation of the two natures, only a union in one hypostasis or person.

The council maintained a clear distinction between the concept of a person and the concept of a nature. Jesus was said to have a divine nature and a human nature while still being only one person; he had everything he needed to be divine and everything he needed to be human (yet without sin). The Second Person of the Trinity did not assume a human person (which is adoptionism) but assumed human nature. The council also made an important distinction, referred to technically as the *anhypostasia/enhypostasia* distinction, which declared that the human nature of Christ did not exist as a person without the divine person of the *Logos* to assume it. While clearly delineating these precise points of theology, the Council of

Chalcedon did not in any way diminish the mystery of the incarnation, of God manifest in flesh.

Relevance

A modern reader who looks at the Definition of Chalcedon is struck by a couple of things right away. First, this is not the way the Bible describes the person of Jesus Christ. The Council of Chalcedon took advantage of extrabiblical ideas to express what they thought Scripture taught. However, it should be kept in mind that the use of different language from Scripture does not mean that there are not biblical principles involved. In many ways, the council and the theological debates leading up to it were driven by an attempt to understand what the Bible says about the person of Jesus Christ. When the Gospels say that Jesus did not know something, this can be explained by the wording of Chalcedon. Jesus' human nature faced the same limitations that all human natures face, including the fact that we are not born knowing everything there is to know. Luke says that Jesus grew in wisdom and knowledge, and this can be understood with the categories provided by the council.

It is also true that Chalcedon is not really a definition as much as it is a set of boundaries. George Lindbeck compares the Council of Chalcedon to a set of grammar rules or rules for a game.[6] If you do not follow the rules, you cannot say that you are playing the game anymore. How do you know how a word functions in a sentence? Through the rules of grammar. Doctrine functions in a similar way. If you go beyond the boundaries that Chalcedon established, you are no longer talking about the person of Jesus Christ, but someone else. Gonzalez says that Chalcedon did not define how the union took place, but "[sets] the limits beyond which error lies."[7] The Definition of Chalcedon is not expected to be an explanation of how God became a man, but rather is a statement of the mystery of faith that has been delivered to us through the prophets and through Christ himself, and in the Creed of Nicaea.

In that sense, it might be helpful to think of Chalcedon as a way to correct extremes in our thinking. Because we sometimes fall into the trap of thinking that Jesus is spiritual and far removed from us, it can be comforting to remember that he is really human. Max Lucado reminds us what it means for Jesus to be truly human in a vivid passage: "Jesus may have had pimples. He may have been tone-deaf. Perhaps a girl down the street had a crush on him or vice versa. It could be that his knees were bony … For thirty-three years he would feel everything you and I have ever felt. He felt weak. He grew weary. He was afraid of failure. He was susceptible to wooing women. He got colds, burped, and had body odor. His feelings got hurt. His feet got tired. And his head ached."[8]

However, against the tendency to think of Jesus as merely human, a wise man, or a spiritual leader, Chalcedon brings to our attention those passages that show his eternal power and glory: "The hair on his head was white like wool, as white as snow, and his eyes were like blazing fire. His feet were like bronze glowing in a furnace, and his voice was like the sound of rushing waters. In his right hand he held seven stars, and coming out of his mouth was a sharp, double-edged sword. His face was like the sun shining in all its brilliance" (Rev. 1:14–16).

How do we reconcile these two seemingly opposite portraits: bony-kneed Jesus and the Holy One of Israel? Chalcedon does not give any illustrations that might help us. But it rules out a number of answers — that the human Jesus is a mask or a fad, or that Jesus is only human except insofar as being human is awkward or embarrassing. The conclusion of the council was that as paradoxical as a God-man might seem, it was important to remember that both portraits show us the same person.

Did Chalcedon satisfy all the questions about the person of Christ? As we will see, it did not. Much of the Eastern church believed that the Chalcedonian definition was too Nestorian and betrayed the simple idea of a single person that Cyril had fought for at Ephesus. In the churches in the West, the question of whether

Christ had two wills or one will was addressed. But this was able to be addressed with less of the drama that surrounded the years preceding Chalcedon because the most important groundwork had been laid.

The Reformers in the sixteenth century accepted the Council of Chalcedon as an authoritative council, and the language of Chalcedon was incorporated into their own creeds and confessions. In the twentieth century, liberal scholars challenged the deity of Christ, but their challenge was rejected by a wide group of Christians, including Catholics, because it violated what the Scriptures teach. When B. B. Warfield wrote about this denial of Christ's divinity in the early twentieth century, he used the language of two natures as an integral part of his argument, in addition to Scripture.[9] That language is taken directly from Chalcedon and the history of the battle for the union of two natures in one person. Chalcedon lives today, more than fifteen hundred years later, because it guides the discussion between two heresies and helps us understand what Scripture says about Jesus Christ, God's own son and the son of Mary.

Without the truths that were expressed in the Definition of Chalcedon, it is difficult to see how our salvation was accomplished. If Christ were not fully human, or if he were not fully divine, he would not be able to serve as our mediator — as the God-man. He would be either just another man or God himself. Rather, as Anselm put it in his famous *Cur deus homo* ("Why God Became Man"), since sin is an affront against God, then a payment from a human will not suffice. The satisfaction of the debt, he said, must come from God himself. However, only humans are guilty of the penalty due for sin. Put simply, humans *ought* to, but only God *can*, make right the wrong done. It is in the person of Jesus Christ, who was fully God and fully man, that this satisfaction was made and our salvation was completely accomplished.

Discussion Questions

1. Which do you think is more problematic: Nestorianism (two natures and two persons) or Eutychianism (one nature)? Why?
2. Do the details of the history and the people that led up to the Council of Chalcedon change your understanding of the Definition of Chalcedon?
3. Without using any of the language of Chalcedon, how would you explain the gospel accounts of Jesus' getting tired or hungry? How does using the language of Chalcedon help you to be able to explain the same thing?
4. What are some examples of how Christians today use language that does not fully follow the Definition of Chalcedon? Does this language lean toward Nestorianism or Eutychianism?

Further Reading

Gonzalez, Justo L. *The Story of Christianity*. Vol. 1. San Francisco: HarperSanFrancisco, 1984.

Grillmeier, Aloys. *The Development of the Discussion about Chalcedon*. Vol. 2, Part 1 of *Christ in the Christian Tradition*. 2nd ed. Louisville: Westminster John Knox, 1987.

Kelly, Joseph F. *The Ecumenical Councils of the Catholic Church: A History*. Collegeville, MN: Liturgical Press, 2009.

CHAPTER 5

ATHANASIAN CREED

Late 400s to Early 500s

Historical Background

Like the Apostles' Creed, the origin of the Athanasian Creed is unknown. As the name suggests, the creed was originally ascribed to Athanasius — the great "father of Nicene orthodoxy" and defender of the divinity of Christ and the doctrine of the Trinity — as early as the ninth century. Athanasius was a general of doctrinal warfare in his day. He was a pastor, preacher, bishop, and theologian, and most especially a leader in the defense of the faith of Nicaea — especially the claim that the Father and the Son are the very same substance (*homoousios*, in Greek).[1] His battles were not without suffering, and he spent as much time banished from his position in Alexandria as he spent in office. Some of his works are still in print today, such as *The Life of Antony*, about a young man who goes out to the wilderness to defeat his demons, and *On the Incarnation*, outlining the ramifications of the bodily incarnation of Christ.[2] Athanasius was a great champion. But he probably had nothing to do with writing this creed.

Since the seventeenth century, the document has been regarded as conclusively non-Athanasian for several reasons. For one thing, Athanasius never mentioned the creed anywhere in his writings. But perhaps more definitively, none of the councils of Constantinople (381), Ephesus (431), or Chalcedon (451) refer to the document, and it assuredly would have been written before then if it came from the pen of Athanasius, who died in 373. According to scholars, the most likely option is that the Athanasian Creed came from the Latin church from St. Augustine's school of thought, in Gaul or North Africa (and as will be seen in the following section, the creed relies not only on Augustine but also on the three councils).[3]

In its earliest references it was not called a "creed" at all, but "The Faith of Athanasius."[4] Like the Apostles' Creed, the statement of faith associated with Athanasius derives its power not from the name ascribed to it but from the truth that it expresses. Even if it was not written by Athanasius, it emerged out of the time of the church fathers and the ecumenical councils. One of the first references to the creed was made by Caesarius of Arles around AD 502, who transcribed the entire creed in a preface to a collection of sermons, "because it is necessary ... that all clergymen, and laymen too, should be familiar with the catholic (i.e., the Christian) faith" so that they could know what to teach and preach as they went about their ministry.[5] By AD 1090, the great medieval theologian Anselm of Canterbury counted the Athanasian Creed on equal par with the Apostles' Creed and the Nicene Creed as part of the *Tria Symbola*, or Three Creeds of the Christian faith.[6]

The creed continued to wield influence during the Reformation. It sits at the beginning of the Lutheran Book of Concord alongside the Apostles' Creed and the Nicene Creed. It is used by several Reformed churches, and it was mentioned approvingly in the Augsburg Confession, the Formula of Concord, the Thirty-nine Articles, the Second Helvetic Confession, the Belgic Confession, and the Bohemian Confession.[7] According to Martin Luther, the Athanasian Creed was "the most important and glorious composition since the days of the apostles."[8] John Calvin considered it one of "the three symbols" that stand forever "in accordance with the Word of God."[9] The great historian Philip Schaff wrote of the Athanasian Creed, "This Creed is unsurpassed as a masterpiece of logical clearness, rigor, and precision."[10] However, it must also be noted that this creed never achieved universal acceptance, as the Greek church rejected one of the creed's assertion about the Holy Spirit.[11]

What can we learn from the Athanasian Creed? Is it hopelessly stuck in its times, waging battles long past about the nature of God and Christ? Or is it relevant today?

Content

The Athanasian Creed consists of forty-two articles, which can be divided into three parts. The first part addresses the Trinity, relying heavily on Augustine's ideas and even quoting some passages of Augustine's *On the Trinity* verbatim (a strong indication that it was not written by Athanasius himself, since Athanasius died when Augustine was a young man, before he converted to Christianity). The second part defends the two natures of Jesus that Chalcedon had explained, summarizing the results of fourth- and fifth-century debates and presenting them in a neatly distilled and lyrical Latin form. The third part of the creed consists of a set of condemnations that assert that any who will be saved must adhere to the teachings of the creed. These statements have left a bad taste in the mouths of some who don't like to see opponents damned, but it must be recalled that all early creeds and confessions contained "anathemas," lists of beliefs rendered unacceptable to Christian conviction by the truths expressed in the very same creeds. The creed itself reads as follows:

> Whosoever will be saved, before all things it is necessary that he hold the catholic faith. Which faith except every one do keep whole and undefiled; without doubt he shall perish

everlastingly. And the catholic faith is this: That we worship one God in Trinity, and Trinity in Unity; Neither confounding the Persons; nor dividing the Essence.

For there is one Person of the Father; another of the Son; and another of the Holy Ghost. But the Godhead of the Father, of the Son, and of the Holy Ghost, is all one; the Glory equal, the Majesty coeternal. Such as the Father is; such is the Son; and such is the Holy Ghost. The Father uncreated; the Son uncreated; and the Holy Ghost uncreated. The Father unlimited; the Son unlimited; and the Holy Ghost unlimited. The Father eternal; the Son eternal; and the Holy Ghost eternal. And yet they are not three eternals; but one eternal.

As also there are not three uncreated; nor three infinites, but one uncreated; and one infinite. So likewise the Father is Almighty; the Son Almighty; and the Holy Ghost Almighty. And yet they are not three Almighties; but one Almighty. So the Father is God; the Son is God; and the Holy Ghost is God. And yet they are not three Gods; but one God. So likewise the Father is Lord; the Son Lord; and the Holy Ghost Lord. And yet not three Lords; but one Lord.

For like as we are compelled by the Christian verity; to acknowledge every Person by himself to be God and Lord; So are we forbidden by the catholic religion; to say, There are three Gods, or three Lords. The Father is made of none; neither created, nor begotten. The Son is of the Father alone; not made, nor created; but begotten. The Holy Ghost is of the Father and of the Son; neither made, nor created, nor begotten; but proceeding. So there is one Father, not three Fathers; one Son, not three Sons; one Holy Ghost, not three Holy Ghosts.

And in this Trinity none is before, or after another; none is greater, or less than another. But the whole three Persons are coeternal, and coequal. So that in all things, as aforesaid; the Unity in Trinity, and the Trinity in Unity, is to be worshipped. He therefore that will be saved, let him thus think of the Trinity.

Furthermore it is necessary to everlasting salvation; that he also believe faithfully the Incarnation of our Lord Jesus Christ. For the right Faith is, that we believe and confess; that our Lord Jesus Christ, the Son of God, is God and Man; God, of the Essence of the Father; begotten before the worlds; and Man, of the Essence of his Mother, born in the world. Perfect God; and perfect Man, of a reasonable soul and human flesh subsisting. Equal to the Father, as touching his Godhead; and inferior to the Father as touching his Manhood. Who although he is God and Man; yet he is not two, but one Christ. One; not by conversion of the Godhead into flesh; but by assumption of the Manhood by God. One altogether; not by confusion of Essence; but by unity of Person. For as the reasonable soul and flesh is one man; so God and Man is one Christ.

Who suffered for our salvation; descended into hell; rose again the third day from the dead. He ascended into heaven, he sitteth on the right hand of God the Father Almighty, from whence he will come to judge the quick and the dead. At whose coming all men will rise again with their bodies; And shall give account for their own works. And they that have done good shall go into life everlasting; and they that have done evil, into everlasting fire. This is the catholic faith; which except a man believe truly and firmly, he cannot be saved.[12]

It is sometimes said that you cannot describe the Trinity without committing some sort of heresy. Either you make God out to be three gods, or you make the three persons (Father, Son, and Holy Spirit) into a sham and pretense. The reason for this is that to speak about God, to speak about the Trinity, is different from speaking about any other thing. God is categorically separate from all other subjects. God is God. And nothing else is. So when we discuss the Trinity, we are peering into what theologians call the "aseity" of God — God as he is a se, to himself. God presents himself fully only to himself. We know about the Trinity only because God lovingly reveals aspects of his being and character to us. But God knows himself very well!

Given these challenges in expressing the great mystery of the Godhead who is "one God in Trinity and Trinity in unity," the Athanasian Creed is about as careful and thorough an attempt as can be found in the history of the church. It not only describes and summarizes the core doctrine of the Trinity but also sets boundaries to prevent potential heresies and misunderstandings from creeping in.[13]

Despite the dense language, the creed is designed to be practical. It begins by recognizing what Christians must believe and whom we must worship. It is essentially a guide to worship, and worship for the purpose of individual right-relatedness to God. This means worshiping one God who is revealed to be Father, Son, and Holy Spirit for "their glory is equal, their majesty coeternal."[14]

The Athanasian Creed then guides the worshiper through key aspects of divinity, qualities or attributes of God, that are shared by all three persons of the Trinity. God is uncreated. God is unlimited. God is eternal. Each person of the Trinity is each of these things, but does that mean that there are three separate divinities? The Father is uncreated. The Son is uncreated. The Spirit is uncreated. Since the creed makes a point of distinguishing each person from each other and since all three are uncreated, doesn't that mean three Gods? The creed answers with the simple formula, which it will repeat throughout, "not three, but one."[15] "In the same way, the Father is almighty, the Son almighty, the Holy Spirit almighty; yet there are not three almighties, but one almighty." The authors of the creed take pains to identify each quality with each person to show their equality, but it is made very explicit that there is only one God. In this way there is no room for tritheism, the suggestion that there are three gods worshiped in Christianity. (This was never a serious suggestion in Christian circles anyway. It was used as a polemic against rival Christian groups.) More important, the creed eliminates a prominent view of the Trinity that was very active, and openly supported throughout the fourth century. This view (sometimes called Neo-Arianism after the original advocate, Arius) was promoted by royalty and bishops alike, and suggested that while the Father, Son, and Holy Spirit were all "God," the Son and then the Holy Spirit certainly had to be regarded as less God than God the Father. Maybe they are God, enough for us to worship them. But not *as* much God as the one true God at the top of the triangle.[16] The Athanasian Creed disallows this view of God. There cannot be multiple Almighties.[17]

Why not just think of God as a single person, if monotheism is the goal? Are the persons of the Trinity simply ways that God chooses to appear to us at various times and for various purposes? There is no room for this misunderstanding, which is sometimes referred to as Modalism because it suggests that God appears to us in different modes; or Sabellianism, after its early advocate Sabellius (exiled in AD 220). Maybe God just appears to us sometimes as Father, sometimes as Son, sometimes as Spirit. The view was untenable because Scripture records and reveals to us interactions between the persons. The Father blesses the Son. The Son prays to the Father. The Son breathes the Spirit. The Father raises the Son from the dead. We do not understand fully how the Father, Son, and Spirit interact, but as the creed teaches, we can say that the Son is "begotten" of the Father. We can say as well that the Spirit "proceeds." (Both of these expressions come from Scripture: Ps. 2:7 and John 15:26 respectively.) The orthodox reading is more difficult to understand than simple monotheism or separating the three persons altogether, but it is most faithful to Scripture.

Relevance

The Athanasian Creed does not add any new interpretations on the Trinity or the nature of Jesus Christ (part of the creed, but not analyzed here) — for the most part, it is a summary of the decisions of the past councils. However, it takes the Trinity seriously. It is refreshingly straightforward in that it challenges the reader to believe these things or face eternal damnation.

Why should we have to believe these particular things to be saved? For centuries, scholars and Christian leaders have expressed their discontent with the confident proclamation that to believe these things is to be saved, but to deny them is to "assuredly perish eternally." A William Chillingworth (1602–44) biographer records that he despised the creed: " ... he could not apprehend, much less affirm, that anybody should perish everlastingly, or be damned, for not believing that exposition. He thought that it was a great presumption thus to confine God's mercies."[18] These sentiments are no strangers to our times. We have a hard time accepting that eternal damnation is the potential result for any human being. This creed serves to remind us of that fact. Even its damnatory clauses are helpful "in the reminder they give of the awful responsibility of making the right decision in matters of fundamental belief."[19] The Christian faith is not only a matter of the heart, an exercise in sentimentality, for "Christian faith is a matter of the mind as well as the heart and the will, and as thinking persons we must give intellectual expression to our faith."[20] Still it does not demand blind acceptance to empty propositions. It is concerned with the direction of our souls. To paraphrase Philip Schaff, the point of the creed is not that we are saved by memorizing a set of statements, but that we are saved by trusting in the one who has revealed himself. Trusting in him, as far as he has told us about himself, is what saves, while straying from him is what condemns.[21] The Athanasian Creed points us to the identity of the one who saves.

Discussion Questions

1. How do you think about the Trinity? Has reading this creed challenged your understanding?
2. Why do you think the Athanasian Creed is so insistent that you have to believe certain things to be saved, and that if you do not believe them, you open yourself up to suffering eternal damnation?
3. Is the creed right to be so insistent on the Trinity? Why or why not?

Further Reading

Behr, John. *The Nicene Faith*. 2 vols. Crestwood, NY: St. Vladimir's Seminary Press, 2004.

Kelly, J. N. D. *The Athanasian Creed*. New York: Harper and Row, 1964.

Studer, Basil. *Trinity and Incarnation*. Edinburgh: T&T Clark, 1993.

Torrance, T. F. *The Trinitarian Faith*. Edinburgh: T&T Clark, 1995.

CHAPTER 6

COUNCILS OF CONSTANTINOPLE
381, 553, 681

Historical Background

As Rome declined in power, the emperor Constantine established a new capital in Greece that he (very modestly) named after himself. Constantinople became the heart of the empire for the next thousand years, and since it had been founded by a Christian emperor, it quickly became the symbol of imperial Christianity. Massive cathedrals such as Hagia Sophia defined the skyline of the city, while famous scholars such as John Chrysostom and Gregory of Nazianzus made pronouncements that spread throughout the entire Mediterranean world. It is perhaps unsurprising that three major councils took place in such a setting, one in 381, a second in 553, and a third in 681.

The issues addressed by these councils varied widely, and although their pronouncements settled important controversies, they are much less well-known than Nicaea or Chalcedon. Constantinople I established the full deity of the Holy Spirit, while Constantinople II and Constantinople III clarified the nature and the divine will of Christ. You might think of these councils as refining the definitions that the church had settled on earlier. Inevitably, the language used in the earlier councils had left more wiggle room than the writers had intended, and these subsequent councils worked to make sure that the original intent was preserved.

It will be useful to clarify a potential point of confusion. The three councils were known as "ecumenical," a term that meant that representatives from all of the branches of the Christian church (both East and West) met and acknowledged the rulings of the councils as authoritative for the life of the church. Because other ecumenical councils occurred in other cities as well, the numbers of the councils of Constantinople do not correspond to their numbers as ecumenical councils. As a point of reference, the First Council of Constantinople (381) was the Second Ecumenical Council of the church; the Second Council of Constantinople (553) was the Fifth Ecumenical Council of the church; and the Third Council of Constantinople (681) was the Sixth Ecumenical Council. In this chapter, however, we will be using only the designations "first," "second," or "third" to avoid confusion.

Constantinople I (381)

In 325, the Council of Nicaea had ruled that Christ was "very God of very God," not merely a created being that God used to create the world, which was what the monk Arius had claimed. Many accounts of church history end here and say that Constantine then Christianized the empire with the sword and forced the Arian Christians to conform to a few orthodox thinkers. However, for the next several decades Roman emperors favored a form of Arianism[1] and persecuted orthodox Christianity. As just one example, when eighty priests petitioned the Arian emperor Valens to reconsider appointing a controversial figure, he is said to have had them set adrift in a boat and burned them to death.[2] While orthodox Christians in 381 no longer had to live in the same fear of mass persecution they had during the previous century, they were still locked in a desperate struggle to preserve their doctrines.

Nicaea had condemned Arianism, but many of the Arians had found a way to conform to Nicaea (more or less) without compromising their key beliefs. Arius had said that Christ was a created being, but some Arians, who were often called Semi-Arians, said that Christ was "like God."[3] In this, they reflected older orthodox language of the church, which had said that Christ was "like God" in order to ward off the objections of those who said that there was no difference between Christ and God the Father. At first, the orthodox faction gave the Semi-Arians the benefit of the doubt and declared that they too were orthodox.[4] However, it quickly became clear that the two groups were indeed separate. The Semi-Arians could agree wholeheartedly with Nicaea that they "believed in the Holy Ghost," which was all that Nicaea had to say about the matter, but they understood the Holy Ghost to be a force or a power, while the orthodox had meant that the Holy Ghost was the Third Person of the Trinity.[5] Consequently, another council was called after the death of Emperor Valens (who, as mentioned above, had been militantly Semi-Arian) in order to settle the matter.

Both sides had ample reason for believing as they did. In order to understand the Semi-Arian position, consider some of the language used of the Holy Spirit in Scripture. A prophecy in Joel 2:28 (and quoted in Acts 2) says: "And afterward, I will pour out my Spirit on all people. Your sons and daughters will prophesy, your old men will dream dreams, your young men will see visions." How does someone "pour out" a person? David prays to God the Father in Psalm 51 not to "take your Holy Spirit from me," which suggests that the Holy Spirit is something that God uses rather than a separate person who acts. In the New Testament, it seems that the Holy Spirit is a way to describe a state of being, as when the disciples are "filled" with the Holy Spirit or the Holy Spirit is "quenched." If these verses are talking about a person, then it would have to be a person like no other, and the Semi-Arian case is strengthened by the fact that neither God the Father nor Jesus are described in these terms.

Moreover, the early church itself varied widely on how it referred to the Holy Spirit. The language of the Spirit as a power was used at early ordinations, for example: "God and Father of our Lord Jesus Christ, Father of mercies and God of all comfort ... Pour forth now that power, which is yours, of your royal Spirit, which you gave to your beloved Servant Jesus Christ, which he bestowed on His holy apostles."[6] A third-century book of liturgy speaks of church as "the place where the Holy Spirit abounds," as though the Holy Spirit were an especially favorable crop.[7] Finally, then as now, the Holy Spirit was referenced less frequently than the Father and the Son, and the theology surrounding the Spirit had been less developed; hence, the Semi-Arians could correctly point to places in the historical tradition that implied the Spirit was an impersonal force that could be predicted, measured, or used.

The orthodox faction had its own Scripture and history to support the idea that the Holy Spirit is a divine person. Despite the verses that suggested that the Holy Spirit is impersonal, theologian Gregory of Nazianzus maintained that the vast majority of the Bible spoke of a personal being. Hence the Holy Spirit could be grieved (Isa. 63:10; Eph. 4:30), as well as lied to (Acts 5:3), and could speak (Mark 13:11),[8] empower (rather than simply *being* a power, Acts 1:8), and console (John 14:16). With respect to history, it had been customary since the earliest times to baptize new believers in the name of the "Father, Son, and Holy Spirit," as an early second-century manual known as the *Didache* attests.[9] Did it make sense, the orthodox theologians asked, to baptize someone in the name of a divine being, a semidivine being, and an impersonal force?[10] Surely the fact that baptisms had to include all three names meant that there was some sort of equality between them. In the early third century, North African theologian Tertullian had explained the meaning behind the triple name by saying that baptism is not a way of gaining a new superpower but the process in which believers purify their bodies so that they would be fit for God to live there: "Not that *in* the waters we obtain the Holy Spirit, but in the water ... we are cleansed and prepared *for* the Holy Spirit."[11] In this view, the Holy Spirit is a person who interacts with us according to his will, rather than ours.

At the time of the first council, the orthodox faction worried most of all that the Semi-Arian doctrine of the Holy Spirit would betray the promise that God himself, rather than a power, would be with us always. The orthodox held that because of Christ's death and resurrection, the gap between a holy God and a sinful human-ity had been bridged, and God himself had come to dwell with us forever. However, the Semi-Arian interpretation leaves us to our own devices — equipped with the Scriptures and a special power given through baptism, we are then responsible for making the long climb to God on our own. Instead, the orthodox party believed that the Holy Spirit was given to us always so that God would guide us to himself. In a sermon to his congregation in Constantinople, Patri-arch Gregory of Nazianzus explained how the Holy Spirit leads us to godliness and salvation: "[He is the one] That reveals, illumines, quickens, or rather is the very Light and Life; That makes Temples; That deifies; That perfects so as even to anticipate Baptism, yet after Baptism [is] to be sought as a separate gift ..."[12] It is notable that many of the Semi-Arians were men of exceptional moral rigor but apparently little gentleness,[13] and although Gregory also exhorted his listeners to focus on doing good works, he reminded them, "God specially rejoices in revealing Himself to the world as Love."[14] The Holy Spirit is the one who provides that love, rather than being a power for morally perfect people to wield.[15]

The council was convened in early 381 by decree of the Emperor Theodosius, but unlike Constantine at Nicaea, he recused himself and left the bishops to their own devices. The council was thus largely free of political pressure and could focus on purely theologi-cal issues, with both sides well represented. The decision of the coun-cil favored Gregory of Nazianzus and the orthodox; consequently, the Nicene Creed was expanded to say, "I believe in the Holy Ghost, the Lord, the Giver of Life, who proceeds from the Father[16] [the Western churches later added 'and the Son'], who with the Father and the Son is worshiped and glorified, who has spoken through the prophets." The revised creed left no wiggle room for the Semi-Arians. The Holy Spirit was now identified as a person who fulfills a role that God had reserved for himself (the Giver of Life, both physical and spiritual), intimately connected with the Father and not a separate deity, who deserves to be the object of worship, and who has been active in salvation from Old Testament times. Constantinople I marked the final ruling on the Arian controversy, and Arianism was finally and officially banned from the church.

Constantinople II (553)

The issue of Christ's nature had largely been settled in the fifth century, at the councils of Ephesus (431) and Chalcedon (451), but controversies continued for centuries to come. The earlier councils had tried to sort out two doctrines: first, that Christ was a single person, but second that he was both fully human and fully divine. As you might imagine, these rulings seemed to contradict one another, and there were large groups that refused to accept these councils outright. In Persia, far to the east, Nestorians (those who believed that Jesus consisted of two persons) who had rejected the decision at Ephesus were gathering force, while all along the Mediterranean coast in Syria, Egypt, Palestine, and farther inland in Armenia were large groups that rejected Chalcedon, known as Monophysites (those who believed that Jesus' humanity was absorbed into his divinity). The church was thus splintered into three large segments, two of which (those who accepted Chalcedon and the Monophysites) lived in the same empire. Constantinople II attempted to reconcile the Chalcedonians and the Monophysites by condemning Nestorius once more and putting the language of Chalcedon into terms that might be more palatable to the Monophysites.[17]

Historian G. L. C. Frank has summarized the Monophysite objections brilliantly: "Nestorius' 'prosopic union' failed to answer very easily the question of who, rather than what, was the subject of the experiences of Jesus of Nazareth."[18] While Nestorius had argued that Christ suffered only in his human nature, the thrust of his opponent Cyril's arguments was that Jesus was a single person who had experienced everything as a whole. Cyril had since become the darling of the Monophysites, the standard by which they measured all pronouncements as orthodox. However, while the bishops had struggled to keep Cyril's emphasis on the unity of Christ at the Council of Chalcedon, they also felt a need to assert that Christ was utterly and completely human as well as being divine. It had been held for centuries that it was vital for redemption that Christ was completely human; as the third century theologian Origen had written: "What was not [taken up] is not saved."[19] Chalcedon tried to retain the emphasis on humanity and divinity in Cyril's single person, and had decided to speak of the two aspects as *natures*, rather than *persons*, to avoid Nestorianism. To the Monophysites, however, the decision at Chalcedon was merely Nestorianism under another name. The Monophysite theologian Philoxenus of Mabbug stated bluntly, "There is no nature without person, just as there is no person without nature. If there are two natures, there must be two persons and two sons."[20] Clearly, there was a need to clarify the decision of Chalcedon further.

Emperor Justinian therefore summoned an ecumenical council in May 553, hoping to reconcile the Monophysites by making clear his dismissal of Nestorianism. The patriarchs from Rome and Constantinople (with a primarily Chalcedonian constituency) as well as those from Alexandria and Antioch (with a primarily Monophysite constituency) were in attendance. Together, they hammered out a compromise that they thought would uphold Chalcedon but alleviate the Monophysite concern that Cyril's theology was being undermined. The record of the council shows a high reverence for Cyril, and frequently cites his arguments as authoritative. The council also deliberately mentions that Christ is a single person, not two, in several places,[21] and specifically condemns those who understand two natures as two persons either in the way that they talk about Christ or in the way that they worship him. The writings of several theologians, such as Theodore of Mopsuestia, were condemned as Nestorian. The extent of the council's reverence for Cyril has led some historians to conclude that Constantinople II was a counterattack by the Monophysites that undid the decision at Chalcedon. At the same time, however, the council was also careful to reinforce the ideas of Chalcedon: Cyril's language was accepted only insofar as it also coincided with Chalcedonian language.[22]

The attempt at reconciliation, regrettably, failed; it simply did not alleviate the concerns of the Monophysite faction sufficiently. To this day, the Syriac Orthodox, Armenian Orthodox, and Coptic Orthodox churches continue to reject Chalcedon. The theological break between the Chalcedonians and the Monophysites eventually became a political break as well, as those provinces that embraced Monophysite Christianity were all swept into the Islamic Caliphate less than a century later.[23] The territories involved represented a significant percentage of Christians at the time, as well as many of the oldest Christian communities.

Constantinople III (681)

Because Constantinople II had not reconciled the Chalcedonians and the Monophysites, a new idea was proposed, called Monothelitism. Monothelitism was a variety of the Monophysite position — it suggested that Christ had only one active will, the divine (*monothelite* is Greek for "only one will"), while his human will was passive. In this way, the proponents of Monothelitism believed, the controversy was resolved. Christ retained two natures and two wills, but since one will was subordinated to the other, there was no question of how Christ had experienced his earthly life as one person. The theory was advocated by a small group of dedicated theologians led by a man named Sergius and heartily endorsed by Emperor Heraclius, who saw Monothelitism as the key to mending the break between Chalcedonians and Monophysites once and for all.

The issue of "one will versus two wills" is perhaps one of the most obscure debates in church history. As mentioned before, several of the early church fathers were concerned that if Christ was not *completely* human, humanity could not be completely redeemed. But Monothelitism does suggest that Christ is completely human, only that his human will was a nonissue in his life. The divine will even governed basic human tasks like eating, drinking, and other material functions.[24] On the surface, it seemed like an ideal compromise between Monophysitism (Christ as a single person is the most important doctrine) and Chalcedonianism (Christ as a single person both fully human and divine is the most important doctrine) because Christ steers both wills with a single rudder.

Ranged against the Monothelite view were the Dyothelites, led by a theologian named Maximus, who maintained that Christ had two wills that worked in concert. Maximus was keen to avoid the error of reducing Christ to several whats instead of a single who — in that respect, he sympathized with the Monothelites. But he held that having two wills did not necessarily mean two wills that conflicted. Instead, Christ needed to add a human will to his divine, preexistent will so that he could bring his humanity into obedience. Christ's human will covered every aspect of his life, including both basic functions and more advanced goals, as he "did not will to drink sour wine, did not want to walk in Judea, did not want anyone to know when he passed through Galilee."[25] But all these human desires were innocent and did not offend God.

Constantinople III, which eventually adopted Maximus's position, phrased the saving cooperation of the wills in this way: "His human will was lifted up by the omnipotency of his divinity, and his divine will was revealed to men through his humanity."[26] Scholar Demetrios Bathrellos puts it like this: "If Christ did not have two distinct wills — namely, a human will next to his divine will — then a basic aspect of our humanity would have been left unassumed, or would have been confused with the divinity, and this would have endangered not only the reality of the humanity of Christ and his consubstantiality with us [in other words, Christ would not have *really* been human as we understand human], but also the reality of our salvation."[27]

To see how the "one will" versus "two will" theories make a difference, consider how a Monothelite theologian, Pyrrhus, and a Dyothelite theologian, Maximus, handle the issue of Christ's suffering. Pyrrhus describes the plea of agony at the garden of Gethsemane as "expressing our nature, which loves life and does not want to die."[28] Christ was not really asking the Father to spare him the cross, Pyrrhus explains, since that would mean that Christ was willing something that the Father did not. Instead, he was empathizing with how one of us would feel in the situation. By way of contrast, Maximus argued that Christ genuinely wrestled with the question of dying, but redeemed our disobedience in Eden by making his human will obedient to the point of death. Pyrrhus's position certainly resolves some potential difficulties with Christ's divinity, especially his relationship to God the Father, but in the final analysis, Christ's life ends up being a sort of sham, where he takes on human experience as though he is playing a part in a play. Thus, the seemingly minor doctrine of "two wills" has real consequence.

Maximus did not live to see his theology vindicated at the Third Council, because he was martyred by a Monothelite emperor in 662.[29] The Third Council of Constantinople was summoned almost twenty years afterward, in 681, and resolved that the doctrine of Monothelitism was anathema. Today, no major group maintains Monothelitism.[30]

Relevance

The three councils of Constantinople were clearly about very different issues, and each has lessons to teach us. Constantinople I showed how necessary it is to submit to God's guidance through the Holy Spirit rather than trying to establish oneself as a sort of spiritual master. To remedy the awkward way of talking about the two natures of Christ, Constantinople II reinforced the idea that Christ is a single person, a who rather than a what, a person who has two natures rather than the sum of a human/divine merger. Constantinople III showed how vital Christ's human will was to our salvation.

Different though they may be, a common thread of "generous orthodoxy" appears throughout all the councils. None of them were free of political intrigue, and the execution of Maximus was a great blow to free theological discussion. All three, however, were interested in maintaining unity as far as it would go. Until the Semi-Arians had made it clear that they could not accept the deity of the Holy Spirit, the orthodox had assumed that the division was simply the result of different, but equally valid, perspectives. Constantinople II attempted to redefine and extend the language of Chalcedon to include those who had objected to it. Constantinople III began out of an attempt to concede even more ground to the Monophysites. What G. L. C. Frank wrote of Constantinople II could be applied to all three: "[Constantinople II] represents an orthodoxy which is inclusive and embracing, rather than exclusivistic. Throughout the history of the church various kinds of 'orthodoxy' have arisen and have degenerated into sectarianism, in part at least because of the unconscious desire on the part of their proponents to exclude and cut off as many people as possible. The orthodoxy of Constantinople II was the exact opposite. It struggled to give the conflicting parties as much theological space as possible without compromising or sacrificing the truth."[31]

However much the fathers wanted a united church, however, they maintained their loyalty to Christ above all. Hence, each council also demonstrated the "orthodoxy" part of "generous orthodoxy." The deity of the Holy Spirit was deemed crucial to salvation, as was the full humanity of Christ. When the emperor favored a theology that might have reconciled political parties but which compromised the truth, the council maintained the truth even though it meant the continued division of Christendom. For modern Christians, the councils can serve as a reminder to extend all possible charity to those who disagree with us, but also to maintain strong views in the face of opposition.

Discussion Questions

1. How do you approach the Holy Spirit in your life? Is he a person to whom you submit, or a force that you try to channel? What Scriptures can you think of that suggest the Holy Spirit is personal and not a force?
2. In addition to guiding us to God, what other roles does the Holy Spirit play?
3. Although the Second Council of Constantinople attempted to reunite Christendom, it failed to do so. To what extent should modern Christians attempt union with each other, and where should we draw the line?
4. Why might it be helpful to maintain that Christ has two wills? What problems does the "two wills" theory present?

Further Reading

Basil the Great. *On the Holy Spirit.* Crestwood, NY: St. Vladimir's Seminary Press, 2001.

Davis, Leo Donald. *The First Seven Ecumenical Councils (325–787): Their History and Theology.* Collegeville, MN: Liturgical Press, 1983.

Frank, G. L. C. "The Council of Constantinople II as a Model Reconciliation Council." *Theological Studies* 52 (1991): 636–50.

CHAPTER 7

COUNCILS OF CARTHAGE AND ORANGE

419 and 529

Historical Background

In the first four centuries of its existence, the church hammered out a firm theology of the Trinity, the person of Christ, and the person of the Holy Spirit, and its attention turned from the nature of God to the relationship between God and humanity. The main questions that confronted it in the fifth through seventh centuries revolved around grace, free will, and the sinfulness of humankind. Although it was now the nature of humanity rather than the nature of God that was the center of church councils, the decisions reached at Carthage and Orange were no less important to the development of Christianity than those at Nicaea and Chalcedon. In fact, the councils defined what scholars term "theological anthropology" — a description of humanity derived from a God-centered worldview. With God in the picture, humanity has a new standard by which to measure itself.

However, while the knowledge of a good and loving God throws a light on how far short humankind can fall, Christian doctrine is complicated by the teaching on Adam's fall from grace. Orthodox Christian doctrine has always been that each human bears responsibility for his or her own sinfulness. The question is, How much responsibility? If sin came into the world through Adam and infected everyone else without their consent, can individuals really be held accountable for sins they commit?

Secular views of humankind sometimes blame the evil in the world on oppressive institutions, bad genetics or upbringing, or psychological disorders. Although these explanations are certainly valid, they can be abused to avoid taking real responsibility for one's actions. The challenge for orthodox Christianity is to agree with these secular views that there is an evil influence beyond our control that has skewed our ability to do good, but to maintain that we bear some responsibility even given this influence, and that there is a great deal that we do that cannot be blamed on anyone but ourselves. Worse, there is a great deal that we do with good intentions that ends up only causing harm.

In the debates at Carthage and Orange, theologians attempted to strike a balance between human responsibility for sin (and human ability to do good) and the doctrine that we live in a fallen world. The debate began with a British monk named Pelagius, who thought he had found a real answer to those who blame evil on our environment rather than ourselves. He advocated a worldview in which humans had full freedom and full responsibility for their actions. If God is just, Pelagius believed, he will punish or reward humans only for the choices that they can freely make, and so he created a world that lets each person choose good and bad however they please. On the other side, a North African bishop named Augustine promoted a view in which humans are born into the bondage of Adam's sin. People are destined to sin more and more unless God intervenes, in which case they are gradually freed to do good by the power of God's Spirit. At Carthage, the council ruled that Augustine's idea was more true to both Scripture and to the human experience than that of Pelagius, even though it was much less palatable. Later, Orange reaffirmed Augustine's teaching against the Semi-Pelagians, those who didn't go as far as Pelagius but still held a more optimistic view of human nature.

Pelagius and the Doctrine of Grace

Pelagius was a British monk who was deeply devoted to living a moral life. When he came to Italy to be a teacher, he was shocked to see how lax the Italian Christians often were. One of their more infamous offenses was a tendency among Italian noblemen to take multiple mistresses in addition to their wives, or to buy slave girls to keep as mistresses, and this was apparently true of both pagans and Christians.[1] Several lived comfortable lives in the midst of great wealth, while the society around them was often desperately poor. The clergy was taking little action to confront these Christians, either allowing them to continue in open sin after baptism without any rebuke or permitting them to remain in a sort of halfway state, as "catechumens" (unbaptized Christians — they could participate in church but not the Eucharist).[2] To Pelagius, the situation clearly violated Christ's teachings. In one of his letters, he wrote, "Do you consider him a Christian who oppresses the wretched, who burdens the poor, who covets others' property, who makes several poor so that he may make himself rich, who rejoices in unjust gains ... and a man of this kind has the audacity to go to church!"[3] Unless a person denied himself and imitated Christ, Pelagius warned, he had no business calling himself a Christian.

Partly from his observations in Italy as well as from his own strictly disciplined life, Pelagius developed a doctrine of sin and salvation that hinged on good works. According to him, sin cannot stem from a preexisting condition, because it would mean that God had created sin as part of human nature: "To say that man cannot be without sin is like saying that a man cannot live without food or drink or sleep or other such things without which our human state cannot exist."[4] Instead, Pelagius taught, sin comes from bad habits that people willingly form. As humans continue to sin, their wills become weaker and bad deeds more frequent, but if they will commit themselves to do good, they can reverse these trends. The role of God in this scheme is threefold: God gives each person free will, the ability to see for themselves what is right and wrong, and revelation through Scripture to guide them.[5] Christ is the ultimate form of grace, the perfect divine guide that God has given humanity to demonstrate the right way. In the end, however, the only thing that matters is whether one has fully eradicated evil from oneself.

To modern ears, Pelagius's ideas might seem self-righteous, a way of setting yourself up to be holier than those around you. Pelagius himself, however, wrote from pastoral concern. He thought that the idea of original sin inherited from Adam — that the world was already crippled by an evil influence — led Christians to be apathetic about their own sins. "Anyone who hears that it is not possible for him to be without sin ... will never do penance appropriate to his misdeeds but will believe that God will lightly remit what rightly he ought not even to impute."[6] (In plain English — if Christians are always going to be sinful and God is just going to forgive sins, what's the motivation to even try to change? Pelagius is suggesting that original sin removes the sense of evil from sin.) Pelagius worried that if the church embraced the idea of original sin, it would inadvertently give Christians an excuse for tolerating their own sins, and that God would judge them harshly on the day of judgment.

Augustine and the Doctrine of Grace

On the other side of the debate was Augustine, a prominent North African bishop who had already weathered many controversies. Only a few years before the Council of Carthage, Augustine had dealt with a splinter group known as the Donatists, who preached that the church should consist only of those who live perfectly holy lives.

In many ways, the Donatists prepared Augustine for the new challenge of Pelagius. Against the Donatists, Augustine had argued that the church does not consist of perfect people (not that he believed there is such a thing) but consists simply of those who have been baptized into the church. He compared the church to the parable of the tares and the wheat in the gospel: "What swelling of arrogance it is, what forgetfulness of humility and gentleness, that any one should dare or believe that he can do what the Lord did not grant even to the apostles — to think that he can distinguish the tares from the wheat."[7] Having dealt with the Donatist disappointment of how the institution of the church looks in real life, Augustine now turned to Pelagius's disappointment with how sinners look in real life.

Augustine firmly believed in original sin. In his view, humans begin life in the grip of a power that they cannot shake, and which will draw them deeper and deeper into destruction unless God himself rescues them. Just as Pelagius's dogmas reflected his own life of self-discipline and hard work, Augustine was influenced by a youth that was wasted in increasingly selfish pursuits. From his point of view, his desires had propelled him into sin, but he had not reformed his life by increasing his desire to do good. In his spiritual autobiography, Confessions, he took the words of Paul in Romans 7 as his watchword: "Even though a person may be delighted with God's law as far as his inmost self is concerned, how is he to deal with that other law in his bodily members [which delivers] him as prisoner to the law of sin dominant in his body. Who will free him from this death-laden body, if not your grace, given through Jesus Christ our Lord?"[8] By these words, Augustine demonstrated how helpless he had been in his former life, and how much he owed to the mercy of God.

If Pelagius had solved the problem of sin and human responsibility by arguing that humans are perfectly capable of doing whatever they want, Augustine solved it by saying that humans deliberately act against the good ideals that they don't know and are selfish, greedy, lustful, stubborn, and proud. In his words, people are *non posse non peccare*, "not able not to sin," because even the good things that we do are not out of love for God but for some lesser purpose. In Augustine's scheme, grace is not a divine nudge but a power that frees people to love God for who he really is. It is this God-empowered love that destroys the rule of sin and bestows the ability to choose to sin or to choose not to sin (*posse non peccare* — "able not to sin"). However, until this grace is given, people cannot choose goodness. Though we might be in the grip of an evil power that we do not understand, we are still responsible for spending our time and energy on the things that we do wrong. Furthermore, he held that all of humankind had committed sin when Adam had — the act of disobedience had been committed together, in a mystical way.[9] As such, there were no innocent victims who had been wronged by a third party — everyone had crippled themselves.

The Council of Carthage (418)

Pelagius and Augustine might never have clashed if the Roman Empire had remained intact. As it was, however, the empire was crumbling, and in 410 Rome itself was sacked by Alaric, king of the Visigoths. The Gothic incursions sent Roman nobles fleeing to fortress towns on the coast and forced Pelagius and his followers across the sea into North Africa. There, a disciple of Pelagius named Caelestius began spreading Pelagian ideas, and it was not long before a synod of African bishops was assembled to deal with the two conflicting visions of God's grace and human free will. The Council of Carthage was assembled early in May 418, and came down heavily on the side of Augustine.

Among the eight canons that the council passed, there are three ideas that pose significant challenges to Pelagius. Two of these are about original sin and free will. First, the council stated that infants require baptism because baptism is not only a symbol but actually washes away sin.[10] This was a practical way of recognizing Augustine's position that humankind is born into sin rather than working itself into sin.

Second, the council decreed that a sinless life was impossible. Over and against the idea that Pelagius and Caelestius had proposed, that the biblical writers called themselves sinners out of humility rather than any real sin, the council reaffirmed the statement in 1 John 1:8: "If we claim to be without sin, we deceive ourselves and the truth is not in us." It was an important recognition that our sins go deeper than we ourselves ever realize. By taking this position, the council was refuting the idea that we are in complete control of what is good or bad in us, and consequently the idea that we can perfect ourselves.

Finally, the council took a stand on the power of God's grace. Pelagius had said that the phrase "God's grace" means that God has given people a natural ability to overcome their sins. The council took a much stronger view of the power of grace and of its role in the relationship between God and humankind: in short, the council stated that grace is primarily related to bringing God and man closer together, "so that we may know what to seek, what we ought to avoid, and also that we should love to do so."[11] Grace is not simply a tool that people can use to conform to certain behaviors but also a description of how God changes people from the inside as well as the outside by helping them love him rather than sin. The council argued that God's grace is something he gives, not something that we choose at our convenience, and that it overpowers the stranglehold sin has on our lives: "Without the grace of God, we can do no good thing."[12] Since the council had also said that God remains distant from the world because of our sins, the presence of grace shows the believer in a very tangible way that God has forgiven us and voluntarily united himself with us again.

The council proceeded without much political excitement compared with the councils at Ephesus or Nicaea. The only exception is the actions of Pope Zosimus, who was impressed by the piety of Pelagius and Caelestius and who strongly urged the African synod to recognize the orthodoxy of the Pelagian party.[13] The Africans politely but firmly refused — they had had several unpleasant dealings with

Roman officials and considered themselves competent to decide such a matter in their own province.[14] After a few months, Zosimus conceded the point.

Partly because it was not ecumenical, however, the council remained open to question. Its decision was not accepted as authoritative in the East, and several Christian theologians felt free to question its rulings. In particular, the council's deep pessimism about human freedom alarmed thinkers who thought that the Africans had gone to extremes in rejecting Pelagianism, and that a more moderate position would serve the same purpose without devolving into fatalism. Thus, a second council was called more than a century later at Orange to resolve some of the more controversial issues at Carthage in a way that would be more binding.

The decision at Carthage left much of the Western Christian world torn. On the one hand, most theologians opposed Pelagius, and they were glad that the council thoroughly defeated his ideas. On the other, there was a growing fear that the council had been influenced by Manichaeanism, a sizeable religion that proposed that humankind is trapped in an utterly evil material world and that the only escape is through the spiritual realm. In comparison with this trapped, fatalistic view, the church had traditionally been optimistic about the ability of humans to choose their own fate. The fact that Augustine had once been a Manichaean and that his ideas were central to the council made the suspicion of Manichaean influence a plausible one. Consequently, theologians such as John Cassian argued that while the intent of the Council of Carthage was good, it left no room for human decision-making, or at least decision-making that had any real meaning. The church in their eyes had become just as fatalistic as the Manichaeans.

Those who questioned Carthage thought (1) that the idea that fallen humans are unable freely to choose good in their unredeemed state is self-evidently false, and (2) that the fatalism implied by the council's ideas about predestination is repugnant and contrary to the teaching of Scripture. Perhaps the most famous of the theologians who called Carthage into question was John Cassian, who argued that human freedom is not in conflict with God's grace and that God's predestination is based on his foreseeing who will freely (by grace) come to faith in Christ. For instance, Cassian cited the story of Zacchaeus from the Gospels.[15] In the story, Zacchaeus is a universally despised tax collector who was desperate to catch a glimpse of Jesus. Since he was a short man, he was forced to climb a tree and wait until Jesus passed by. John Cassian argued that God did not cause Zacchaeus to climb the tree — he decided of his own accord to do so, and Jesus rewarded his initial step of faith. Zacchaeus made a decision of his own free will and God responded to that decision — two separate beings treating each other with dignity, rather than one using the other as a puppet.

Unfortunately, in the seventeenth century these "dissenters" from the decision at Carthage were labeled Semi-Pelagians, which links them much closer to the Pelagian heresy than they actually were. Indeed, calling these theologians Semi-Pelagians is much akin to calling those who lived in post–World War II Germany Semi-Nazis, strictly on the basis of their historical location. Regarding the fate of this "Semi-Pelagianism," church historian J. N. D. Kelly notes, "It suffered, inevitably, but unjustly, from a suspected bias to Pelagianism, but what chiefly sealed its fate was the powerful and increasing influence of Augustine in the West."[16]

A second council was called in 529 at Orange in southern Gaul (modern-day France) to deal with these questions. It decided once more in favor of Augustine (who was now deceased). In fact, Augustine's influence was so prevalent that many of Orange's rulings used his language word for word.

Twenty-five canons were passed that ruled out the arguments of those who questioned Carthage. They frequently accused the opponents of the council of having been unknowingly influenced by Pelagius, perhaps as a counterpoint to the accusations that the Council of Carthage had been unknowingly influenced by the Manichaeans. However, while it might be thought that the council was simply called to reaffirm Augustine's teaching, some of the canons acknowledge that free will is a mystery, and in fact Augustine's doctrine of predestination to hell was ruled as heretical.[17] For instance, the council affirmed that free will is restored by baptism (Conclusion) and that Christians have a duty to pray and to persevere in good works (Canon 10). But it was adamant that the will has to be freed by God first before someone can choose to love him: "The love with which we love God … is wholly a gift of God to love God. He who loves, even though he is not loved, allowed himself to be loved. We are loved, even when we displease him, so that we might have means to please him" (Canon 25).[18]

Relevance

Despite the fact that Pelagianism was never widespread, the ideas of Pelagius are compelling and deserve a carefully thought-out response. You might say that Pelagianism is wrong in its denials but challenging in its assertions; in many ways, it seems to answer certain questions about Christianity much more satisfactorily than the rulings at Carthage. For instance, there is no problem about whether God is fair, or of salvation outside of the church, or of the way that leads to heaven. Good people do good things and are rewarded; bad people do bad things and are punished. Any bad person can become a good person if they will only pull themselves up by their bootstraps.

Like most heresies, however, Pelagianism provides easy and attractive answers at great cost. Though Pelagius's God seems more fair, he is certainly much less intimate. The wonder of salvation for Augustine was that God loved him when he was deeply in sin. Rather than waiting until Augustine had gotten his act together and freed himself from sin, God broke into Augustine's life on his own timing and with a scandalous disregard for whether Augustine was a good person. The question of original sin, which seems far removed from everyday life, becomes much more real when applied to those who are trapped in sin. Their fate hung in the balance at the Council of Carthage — whether they would be told to simply get their act together, or told that they were loved first in spite of themselves, and that because of God's love they would be given the ability to conquer sin. At the same time, Pelagius's critiques about leading a holy life and not using grace as an excuse to sin should ring strongly in a consumer culture that often takes it for granted that God should be conforming to its preferences. David Wells, a Protestant cultural critic, once wrote, "Pagans were deathly afraid of the gods and goddesses ... By contrast, we feel that the sacred will be pleased to have us, will spread out the welcome mat, so to speak, and will be grateful for our attention."[19] For all the faults in his theory, Pelagius reminds us that we should not take advantage of God's mercy.

As for the case of those who questioned Carthage, the ruling at Orange is more ambiguous. Some today question how firmly we should hold the rulings at Orange and Carthage at all. They were not ecumenical councils of the church; that is, they were not universally affirmed by the Eastern and Western branches of the church. In addition, some argue that the councils were so concerned with Pelagianism that they ruled out legitimate understandings of the grace of God and human salvation. Today, we can broadly consider both sides at Orange as orthodox, since there are several threads that unite both those who sided with Augustine and those who wanted to avoid the heresy of Pelagius without sacrificing legitimate expressions of human freedom. Most important, both sides absolutely affirmed "that humanity's present condition does not correspond to God's ultimate purpose and original intention in its creation."[20] Moreover, they agree that humans are responsible for their condition, and that God is ultimately responsible for reversing the curse and restoring that which has been broken. Put differently, both sides affirm the crucial doctrine that salvation is by grace alone; nothing that humans can do could warrant their acceptance before a holy God.

Discussion Questions

1. In your everyday life, do you tend to view God's grace as a tool to help you overcome problems, or as a way that God builds a relationship with you? Are these views mutually exclusive?
2. If Christ is a divine guide, what purpose might the crucifixion have for Pelagius?
3. In your opinion, does the influence of original sin detract from our responsibility for sinful actions? Why or why not?

Further Reading

Augustine. *The Confessions*. Translated by Maria Boulding. New York: New City Press, 2001.

Burns, Patout J. *Theological Anthropology*. Sources of Early Christian Thought. Philadelphia: Fortress, 1981.

Chadwick, Henry. *The Church in Ancient Society: From Galilee to Gregory the Great*. Oxford: Oxford Univ. Press, 2001.

"Council of Carthage (A.D. 419)." *Http://www.newadvent.org/fathers/3816 .htm*, accessed May 26, 2013.

"Council of Orange, The." *Http://www.fordham.edu/halsall/basis /orange.txt*, accessed May 26, 2013.

Rees, B. R. *Pelagius: Life and Letters*. Woodbridge: Boydell Press, 1991.

CHAPTER 8

COUNCIL OF TRENT
1545–63

Historical Background

Zoom forward more than a thousand years. If we were watching Europe through a time-lapse camera, we would see civilization contract sharply, then expand again. Roman cities shrink and fall into disrepair. The tribes that had been kept north of the Roman borders move west and south, building forts and dividing up land. Christianity spreads to England, Ireland, and Scandinavia, and Irish missionaries spread the gospel to the remaining pagan lands. Vast armies of Crusaders make their way to the Holy Land and carve out kingdoms, which soon collapse again into Muslim hands. The knowledge of stoneworking that the returning Crusaders bring back leads to the building of stone castles, monasteries, and churches. Nations form, with roads, bridges, industries, and professional armies. Columbus sets out from Spain and finds a whole new world.

Christianity has never been so pervasive. By the end of the Middle Ages, a series of Crusades in Eastern Europe brings the last pagan lands into the Catholic fold, and the Catholic Church seems to hold complete sway over what is now called Christendom. Christian tenets are a part of the hearts and lives of almost all Europeans. Although Old Rome is now long gone, the church has dubbed a huge section of Central Europe (mostly modern-day Germany) as its successor, the Holy Roman Empire.

However, there are signs that Christendom is beginning to crack. In 1453, Muslim Turks conquer Constantinople, the center of Orthodox Christianity, and begin to advance as far as modern-day Austria. Fears that heretics and witches might threaten Christendom result in expanded powers for the Inquisition, which enters the height of its influence. The papal office is occupied by a series of corrupt popes, including Julius the Warmonger, who leads personal armies into battle, and Alexander VI, who hosts orgies at the papal palace. Priests are likewise reputed to be corrupt and illiterate, while both church services and the Bible are available only in Latin. Although there are several attempts to reform the church by introducing more pious clergy and Bibles in the language of everyday people (most notably by Jan Hus, William Tyndale, and John Wycliffe), the church hierarchy reacts with hostility, and these reforms are thwarted.

In 1517, the efforts at reform finally yield fruit. A theology professor named Martin Luther nails a list of demands for reform known as the Ninety-five Theses to the door of the church in Wittenberg, thus setting off a movement that endures. Luther is infuriated by the Catholic practice of "indulgences," a promise that the church will secure forgiveness for those already dead and suffering in purgatory (see the next section) — if people will just contribute some money to the church. The issue of indulgences leads Luther to list further complaints, mainly theological. He feels that with its claims to hold divine authority, the Catholic Church is holding Christians hostage — they can never be quite perfect enough, quite forgiven enough, and so they are always left hoping that the church will be merciful to them and spare them from hellfire. Luther's counterpoint is that Christ does not hold out forgiveness and goodness just a little ways out of reach as something to work toward but brings forgiveness and holiness down to the believer. Protected by powerful supporters, Luther's ideas spread rapidly through the Holy Roman Empire (modern Germany).

By the 1540s, all attempts on the part of the emperor of the Holy Roman Empire to bring about peace between the growing Protestants (Luther did not want anyone to be called Lutherans) and the Catholic Church have failed. The best attempt, the Colloquy at Regensburg in 1541, achieves agreement on justification (how sinful people are reconciled to a holy God) but fails to bring unity to the issue of the authority of the pope and church tradition. But even the agreement on justification rings hollow when the compromise is rejected by both Luther and Rome. Emperor Charles V's long-desired peace between the two factions of his kingdom never materializes.

The challenges brought by the Protestant Reformers force the Roman Catholic Church to recognize that there are serious issues that need to be addressed. Some tend to view the period of reform that took place in the Roman Catholic Church during the middle of the sixteenth century as nothing but an attempt to squelch the fire started by the Protestants, but this is far from what actually happened. Whether one refers to this period as the Counter-Reformation, the Catholic Reformation, or Early Modern Catholicism, the Catholic Church felt the need to respond to the Reformers, clarify its doctrine and vision, and get its institutional politics back on a track that served the church's mission. Put simply, the reforms of the Catholic Church in the middle of the sixteenth century were much more than anti-Protestant polemics; they were a genuine attempt to achieve doctrinal and institutional clarity — albeit with many political and social factors bound up with the church's efforts.

In order to make these reforms, the Catholic Church convenes the Council of Trent, which is held in three stages over the period between 1545 and 1563. As early as 1536, Pope Paul III expresses desire for a church council to meet, but his desires are ignored. This is mostly because even in 1536 the Protestant Reformation is still in its infancy: the Augsburg Confession (Lutheran) is formally presented to the emperor in 1530, Philipp Melanchthon's *Apology of the Augsburg Confession* is written in 1531, and John Calvin writes the first edition of his *Institutes of the Christian Religion* in 1536.

The council inadvertently gains an air of neutrality when political motives lead to the Council of Trent being held in a strictly neutral location. Charles V, the emperor of the Holy Roman Empire, strongly desires some sort of solution to the religious problem in his empire, which is constantly under threat from Muslim invaders. His many efforts on this front include an attempt to have the council in Germany appease the Lutherans with a promise of the reform that they claim to want. However, the pope wants to have the council somewhere in the Papal States in Italy, preferably close to the Vatican so that he can insure his influence is felt.[1] However, the French are not going to attend any council that is held in the Papal States. Finally, the little town of Trent in northern Italy, which is on the cultural border between Italy and Germany, is agreed to, and even though the cardinals are not happy with the accommodations, Trent proves to be satisfactory for all involved.

Since one issue that led to the Council of Trent is the exact boundary of the pope's authority, there is some internal discussion regarding what role the pope will play at Trent. The pope believes he is above the rulings of the council, such that he has the power to veto any decrees of the council. Many of the cardinals and bishops agree with such strong papal authority. On the other side is a group of leaders called the Conciliarists, who believe that the decisions of a council are binding on the whole church, including the pope. This means that the pope will be forced to agree with the conclusions of the council. The pope seeks to avoid such an outcome at all costs, and in the end the council ends up strengthening the pope's authority in relation to the councils.[2]

The Council of Trent is formally called to order on December 13, 1545. "In attendance for the opening session were four archbishops, 22 bishops, and five generals of religious orders along with three papal legates, Cardinals Giovanni Maria del Monte and Marcello Cervini, who were both future popes, and Cardinal Reginald Pole, who was to depart early because of ill-health."[3] Over the next eighteen years, the council meets in three periods, including a ten-year hiatus, ending its work with a 235 to one vote to send the decrees and canons of the council to the pope (who by this time is Pius IV) for his approval.

The Council of Trent

The Council of Trent aimed to remedy the problems within the Catholic Church that had contributed to the Reformers' cries of protest. The reforms included correcting abuses of power by the clergy, clarifying the balance of authority between Scripture and church tradition, and issuing official statements on justification, the sacraments, and purgatory. All in all, the Council of Trent did not repair the fractures between the Catholics and Protestants, but it did succeed in clarifying the Catholic Church's position on significant areas of doctrine and bringing moderate reform to the abuses of power against which the Reformers had revolted.

Institutional/Clergy Reform

Because the Reformers had initially revolted against the abuses of power within the Catholic Church, Trent attempted to straighten out these problems. For instance, whereas bishops before the Reformation could hold office in more than one location (a practice known as pluralism), Trent ruled that under normal circumstances bishops were to be resident and involved in the pastoral ministries of their own dioceses alone. (This cut down on power grabs and forced the bishops to focus on their assigned flocks.) Also, in discussing the sacrament of Holy Orders, or ordination, the Council of Trent specified what qualities should be evident in the lives of priests, which can be seen as an attempt to resolve the moral laxity Luther had seen among them when he visited Rome. Moreover, the council called for each bishop to create a seminary for the training of clergy. This was one of the longest-lasting reforms that the council passed, resulting in more educated clergy who would be better able to serve in their pastoral duties to their congregations.

The most important institutional reform was related to the selling of indulgences (forgiveness for money). Without admitting that Luther was right, the council encouraged the pope to reform the practice of indulgences. While they were still considered a valid form of penance, the church acknowledged that the rampant abuse of the sales of indulgences needed to end.

Scripture and Tradition, and Revelation

The Reformers had decided that the church hierarchy could no longer be trusted. Henceforth, they established the position of *sola Scriptura* ("Scripture alone"), meaning that Scripture is our only ultimate authority for faith and practice. This doesn't mean that the Bible is the only place where truth is found, but it does mean that everything else we learn about God and his world, and all other authorities, are subordinate to the Scriptures. The Scriptures are the sole necessary and sufficient source of our theology.

In contrast, Trent ruled that Scripture *and* tradition were to be given equal weight in determining what Christians ought to believe. The council decided that in addition to the Scriptures stood "also the traditions, whether they relate to faith or to morals, as having been dictated either orally by Christ or by the Holy Ghost, and preserved in the Catholic Church in unbroken succession."[4] This is in contrast to the Protestants, who wanted to give the final and arbitrating authority to the Scriptures alone.

In addition, the Reformers had insisted that only those books that were to be found in the Hebrew Bible could be considered the legitimate Old Testament. This was a departure from early Christianity, which had used a Greek version of the Old Testament that had included several additional books known as the Apocrypha (some of these are: 1 and 2 Maccabees, the Book of Sirach, the Book of Wisdom, and the Book of Tobit). Trent affirmed the Apocrypha as part of the Bible[5] and took up the issue of the Protestant trend of printing Bibles in the vernacular. The council did not directly forbid the translation of the Bible into other languages but declared that the Latin Vulgate was sufficient for the determination of doctrine. Furthermore, it decreed that no edition of Scripture could be made without the permission of the church, reinforcing the penalties that came with printing or owning unauthorized Bibles (thus effectively forbidding translation anyway).[6]

Justification

The most significant doctrinal issue addressed at Trent was the issue of justification, or how a sinful person is reconciled with a holy God who cannot stand sin. Luther argued that we are saved solely through faith in Jesus Christ because of God's grace and Christ's merit alone. We are neither saved by our merits nor declared righteous by our good works. We do not deserve grace, or else it wouldn't be grace. This means that God grants salvation not because of the good things we do, or even our faith — and despite our sin. God's election is the unconditional and unmerited nature of his grace.

Luther further taught that all humans are sinful and sinners, and that Christ is the only one who is good and righteous. As humans, we inherited from Adam a nature that is in bondage to sin. We are born in sin. We are naturally enemies of God and lovers of evil. We needed to be made alive (regenerated) so that we could even have faith in Christ. All of this is grace that we don't deserve. Because we didn't earn or attain this grace, we cannot lose it. God graciously preserves us and keeps us. When we are faithless toward him, he is still faithful.

We can stand before God only by his grace as he mercifully attributes to us the righteousness of Jesus Christ and attributes to him the consequences of our sins, which were judged on the cross. Declaring sinners righteous based on the work of Christ is called the doctrine of "imputed righteousness" — God declares a believer to be good, and even though the believer is not good in reality, this declaration is all that matters.

Because salvation is entirely a work of the Lord, the believer does not have to constantly worry about the state of his or her soul. If salvation is genuine, God will gradually make the sinner obedient to God's commands, but it is a slow process that one never really completes.

The Catholic position was that of "infused righteousness" — God offers to the believer the opportunities and the strength to be good, and it is up to the believer to respond to God on a case-by-case basis. The result is that as the believer responds, his thoughts and habits gradually shape him into the person that God wants him to be. As you might imagine, Luther's position was based solely on faith — trust in God, and he will do the rest — while the Catholics argued that faith is all too often boxed away into a set of ideas, and that the faith that God is looking for needs to be grounded in practical, concrete responses.

The decree on justification took nearly six months to produce and was the longest decree of the council. Part of the problem was that many in the council were somewhat sympathetic to the arguments of the Reformers. Ultimately, however, the attitude at Trent was not amenable to compromise with the Protestants. In the end, the decree on justification clearly defined the Catholic position over against the Protestant principle of *sola fide* (faith alone). The Catholic Church believed that the Reformers had misunderstood both Augustine and the New Testament emphasis on works in advancing a position of justification by faith alone.

The Catholic position on justification has several significant features. First, it might surprise those who think that Catholicism is based on good works that the council asserted that only God can justify. Humans cannot save themselves, but they can prepare themselves for justification.[7] They do this by "freely assenting to and cooperating with" the quickening and helping grace of God; in responding in this way, they "convert themselves to their own justification."[8] In speaking this way, the council preserved the Catholic idea that humans are not able to bring about their own justification without the grace of God, but neither are they merely passive.

The council is explicit that the term "justification" meant a gradual progression rather than a one-time event. By engaging in good works, the believer moves farther and farther away from sin and becomes a truly new creature.[9] The main objection that Trent presents to the Protestant position, that by faith a person can be saved from sin, is that merely believing in Christ does not shape a person into the sort of new creature that God desires: "For faith, unless hope and charity be added thereto, neither unites man perfectly with Christ, nor makes him a living member of His body. For which reason it is most truly said, that Faith without works is dead and profitless."[10]

The council also rejected the Reformation idea that a believer can know for sure that they are saved and destined for eternity with God. This did not mean that the merits of Christ were in some way insufficient, but as a person "considers himself and his own weakness and indisposition, [he] may have fear and apprehension concerning his own grace, since no one can know with the certainty of faith, which cannot be subject to error, that he has obtained the grace of God."[11]

Finally, while Luther and the other Reformers said that good works are the result of being declared righteous by God rather than something that God requires before accepting a believer, the council decreed that believers have not only the ability to do good works, but that good works are part of entering into eternal life. The doctrine of purgatory was formalized as an official church teaching, indicating that the work of becoming righteous continued even after death.

Church and Sacraments

The sacraments were another significant issue discussed at Trent.[12] The Protestant claim that there are only two sacraments was rejected; instead, the council officially upheld seven sacraments: baptism, confirmation, the Eucharist, marriage, penance, extreme unction, and Holy Orders. The council also confirmed that the sacraments convey God's grace to recipients in and of themselves, regardless of the attitude or morality of the recipients or the priest administering them.[13]

Baptism was deemed to be necessary for salvation and to be administered to children; rebaptism, generally meaning baptism of adult believers as practiced by the Anabaptists, was forbidden.

Confirmation was an anointing with oil, signifying a christening by the Holy Spirit, to be administered near adolescence by the bishop.

With regard to the Eucharist (also known as the Lord's Supper — the bread and wine received by believers in a worship service), the council addressed the Catholic/Protestant disagreement on Christ's presence in the bread and wine. Trent approved the term "transubstantiation," which "meant that at the consecration during the Mass, the substance of the bread and wine was changed into the substance of the body and blood of Christ,"[14] even though the outward appearance of the bread and wine remained unchanged. The term transubstantiation was an attempt to explain the mystery of what the Roman Catholic Church believes takes place during the Eucharist.

Another divisive issue in relation to the Eucharist was addressed by the council at this time: whether to continue the practice of offering to laypeople the bread only and reserving the wine for priests, or to allow, as the Protestants all insisted, that both the bread and the cup should be offered to everyone. The council argued that it was up to the church to distribute the sacrament as it pleased, although it acknowledged that the pope might change the policy.[15]

The council also discussed in detail the controversial issue of the sacrament of penance. If Christ died for our sins on the cross, why perform penitential acts for sin? First, the council affirmed the traditional order of penance: the person who came for confession had to be contrite, but perfect contrition was not necessary. (Perfect contrition means being sorry for having damaged the relationship with God, but a person who was sorry for his sins out of fear of punishment would also be forgiven.) The confession to the priest had to be auricular (told to the priest), complete (sin and circumstances), and secret (confessors were bound to secrecy). The basis for this practice was John 20:23: "If you forgive anyone's sins, their sins are forgiven; if you do not forgive them, they are not forgiven." After confession, a work of satisfaction is assigned by the priest after the priest absolves a person of his sin. This work is not meant to atone for sin. (Notice that the sin proper has already been forgiven through the power of Christ.) However, penance is necessary for the progressive justification mentioned earlier. It balances out the evil effects that sin has on the believer so that he is equipped for holy living.[16] Penance was meant to be a practical solution to sin; without these works of satisfaction, the believer is likely to fall into greater sin and incur a greater punishment on the day of judgment.

Marriage was also formalized as a sacrament of the church. The council said that for marriage to be valid, it had to take place in front of two witnesses and the local priest, ending the practice of "clandestine marriages." A clandestine marriage was a private vow of sexual fidelity between a man and a woman, usually peasants. It was customary to pay a fee to be married,[17] and the bride's family was usually expected to provide a dowry, which put marriage out of reach for poorer people. Private vows bypassed the financial issues and (seemed to) achieve the same purpose. However, on a religious front, the Protestants were now challenging the idea of marriage as a sacrament of the church rather than a natural gift of God, and on a social front, the private vows could be given up at any time, resulting in broken families and serial partners.[18] By reinvesting marriage with sacred implications, Trent was hoping to counter both of these problems.

Besides sacraments, the council also formalized church teaching on images and the veneration of saints. Images are material objects (statues, portraits, and so forth) which Protestants said were idols, just as images were in Israel. However, the church claimed that these objects are not to be worshiped as idols were but point to a spiritual reality beyond themselves. In a similar vein, Protestants were concerned that the medieval practice of praying to saints deprived God of the worship he deserved — especially since saints often had their own areas of control, like protecting travelers or finding lost things. In response, the church said that since Christ has only one body, those who had died and gone to heaven were in no way cut off from their brothers and sisters still on earth.

Reception and Influence

The task of implementing the reform measures in the church fell to the pope based on his interpretation of the council. As a result, the authority of the pope actually increased over the coming years.

One of the most lasting influences of the council was the creation of the Roman missal, the books which were used in worship by all Catholic churches until the 1960s. The missal created a formalized liturgy, but also gave the impression that the liturgy could not be changed or altered. The Tridentine (of or relating to Trent) catechism was also created during this period as a means of instruction in the teachings of the church. Similar to the confessions of Protestantism during the time, the Tridentine catechism sought to bring the doctrine of the Catholic Church to common churchgoers. The task of teaching the catechism fell to the local priest, who was to teach the catechism every Sunday and on feast days. In this and other ways, the clergy were now expected to be more pastorally involved in their parishes.

Relevance

Trent revitalized the Catholic Church and corrected a number of abuses. Through Trent, Catholicism regained its power in many of its former lands and was prepared for the great missionary endeavors in the New World, Africa, and Asia. Not long thereafter, the Catholic Counter-Reformation was able to show that real progress had been made and earned back a great deal of the trust that had been lost through decades of corruption. There is little doubt that the church that emerged after Trent was more educated, better equipped to meet the needs of its flock, and much more focused on piety. Nevertheless, the Protestants did not return to the Catholic fold.

When we consider today the many divisions in Christianity, it is apparent that Jesus' prayer "that all of them may be one" (John 17:21) has not yet been answered. The fact that Christians often fight with one another and have even launched wars against one another is not lost on the outside world, and our lack of unity certainly hurts our witness. The Catholic solution, which is to put all Christian groups under the authority of Rome, is increasingly suggested, and if we reject that solution, it is important to know why, because continued division comes with a steep price. What motives could the Protestants have had to keep the church divided, and do we find those reasons compelling?

The Reformers wanted to see Christians living without fear that the church could take away the salvation that properly belongs to God, and to understand that while God requires good works and obedience and reverence from us, he himself comes down to heal us even while we are sinful. They wanted the Bible to be a way in which ordinary people could communicate with God and know God, not just as a sacred object reserved for the most holy. (Remember that since the Bible was in Latin, only priests could read it.) Although Catholicism also sought to meet many of these needs in its own way, the Reformers did not agree that the Catholic Church met them adequately, and the decisions at Trent did not satisfy Protestant objections.

It is fair to ask, Since Trent was in part a firm response to the Protestant Reformation, does it have anything to offer other Christian traditions outside of Roman Catholicism? First, Protestants can acknowledge with Trent the importance of tradition in understanding what Christians ought to believe. Both Catholic and Protestant scholars can enjoy the resurgence of the study of the early church fathers as a shared heritage.

Similarly, while Protestants disagree with Catholics on the doctrine of justification by faith, they can, with Trent, declare anathema the following proposition: "That man can be justified before God by his own works, which are done either in the strength of human nature or through the teaching of the law, apart from the divine grace through Jesus Christ."[19] While the Catholic Church has not changed their decree on justification, the centuries have provided ample opportunity to resolve miscommunication. In 1999 the Catholic Church and the Lutheran World Federation signed the Joint Declaration on the Decree of Justification, in which they agreed on the issue where they could and acknowledged each other's misgivings where they could not, depicting each other fairly and in the best possible light.[20]

In another way, Trent helps us to think out the differences between Protestantism and Catholicism. Is marriage a natural gift of God, for instance, or a special grace given to the church? What were the issues that made the Protestants break away from the church, and were they right? We should definitely not look for reasons to divide those who are called Christians, but there may be issues that are worth disagreeing over (with the humility that most things are a mystery). Trent gives the Catholic answer for those issues and is worth learning for that reason.

Discussion Questions

1. Thinking about the Council of Trent as a reform movement in the Catholic Church, what stood out to you or surprised you about the council's efforts?
2. What do you think would have been different about the Catholic Church's efforts to reform doctrine and practice if the Protestant Reformation had not taken place?
3. What do you think is the importance of Christian tradition and other historical interpretations of the Bible when it comes to understanding the Bible for yourself?
4. How does the Catholic Church's teaching on justification differ from your own understanding? How is it similar?
5. How do you think knowing more about the Council of Trent might help you in your interactions with Catholics?

Further Reading

Bireley, Robert. *The Refashioning of Catholicism, 1450–1700.* Washington, DC: Catholic Univ. Press, 1999.

Bokenkotter, Thomas. *A Concise History of the Catholic Church.* New York: Image Books, 1977, 2004.

Kelly, Joseph F. *The Ecumenical Councils of the Catholic Church: A History.* Collegeville, MN: Liturgical Press, 2009.

Schroeder, H. J., trans. *The Canons and Decrees of the Council of Trent.* Charlotte: TAN Books and Publishers, 1978.

A copy of the Decrees and Canons of the Council of Trent can be found at *http://history.hanover.edu/texts/trent.html*.

CHAPTER 9

HEIDELBERG CATECHISM
1563

Historical Background

By the middle of the sixteenth century, several different strands of the Protestant Reformation had begun spreading like wildfire across the European continent. The diversity within Protestantism proved to be a double-edged sword. Unlike Roman Catholicism, which had established a solid core of beliefs at the Council of Trent, Protestants were only loosely bound together by the five famous "solas" — from the Latin word *sola*, meaning "alone" or "only." The five solas are five phrases or slogans that emerged during the Protestant Reformation and that summarize the Reformers' basic theological convictions that the Reformers believed to be essentials of the Christian life and practice. The five solas are:

1. *Sola Scriptura* ("Scripture alone"): Scripture alone is our highest authority.
2. *Sola Fide* ("faith alone"): we are saved by grace alone, *through faith alone.*

3. *Sola Gratia* ("grace alone"): we are saved *by grace alone*, through faith alone.
4. *Solus Christus* ("Christ alone"): Christ alone is our Lord, Savior, and King, and the only mediator between God and humanity.
5. *Soli Deo Gloria* ("glory to God alone"): we live for the glory of God alone.

These basic beliefs emerged in the Protestant effort to distinguish itself from the teaching of the Roman Catholic Church. On a positive note, this allowed the movement to gain traction quickly in a variety of different contexts and locations, but unfortunately it also meant that disputes and disagreements frequently arose between the different branches of the newfound Protestantism.

Disagreement between the Lutheran and Zwinglian (a group of Protestants founded by Swiss Reformer Ulrich Zwingli) factions was particularly intense. One pointed conflict broke out in Heidelberg under the rule of Otto Heinrich (1556–59) concerning Christ's presence in the Lord's Supper. The Lutherans believed that Christ's body is really present in the bread and wine in the same way that heat permeates an iron placed in a hot fire. In contrast, the Zwinglians believed that the Lord's Supper is primarily a symbolic service of remembrance. Since Christ's body is at the right hand of the Father in heaven, the Zwinglians found it hard to believe that Christ's body could be a real human body and somehow be present both in heaven and in the bread and the wine. (The Calvinists, by contrast, held a third position: they maintained that Christ is present not in body but in Spirit.) One staunch Lutheran fought for making Lutheranism the official religion of the city, and he even went so far as to excommunicate a Zwinglian deacon after getting into a fight over the communion cup with the deacon at the altar.

Because politics and religion were closely related in pre-Enlightenment Europe, it was difficult to just "agree to disagree." So when Frederick III succeeded Otto Heinrich in ruling the city of Heidelberg, he charged the theology faculty to develop a new catechism to lay to rest the often-heated debates over the Lord's Supper and at the same time provide a tool for teaching all of the basic doctrines of the broadly Reformed Protestant faith. The Heidelberg Catechism served as a rallying point for Protestantism, around which the various Protestant denominations could gather in agreement. Because the Heidelberg Catechism both captured the essence of Protestant theology but still managed to avoid being vague or general, it became one of the most famous documents of the Protestant Reformation.

Content

At the time of the writing of the Heidelberg Catechism, catechisms were not terribly common. Martin Luther wrote his first catechism in 1528 and is often credited with being the father of the modern catechism, even though he relied heavily on the previous work of the Bohemian Brethren.[1] The Genevan catechisms, written by Calvin and Guillaume Farel, served as the only other major international catechisms in use prior to the Heidelberg Catechism.[2] Indeed, the Heidelberg Catechism's view of the Eucharist is clearly influenced by the developing Calvinist position as a third way between the Lutheran and Zwinglian stalemate.

The Heidelberg Catechism differs from Luther's Small Catechism (1529) and the Shorter Westminster Catechism (1647) in both tone and content. It aimed both to provide a guide for the religious instruction of the city's youth as well as to provide a unified confession of faith for the newly formed Protestant church. As a document intended to squelch conflict rather than draw lines in the sand, the Heidelberg Catechism is the most inclusive of all the Reformed confessions; as Philip Schaff puts it, the Reformed doctrine of the catechism "is herein set forth with wise moderation, and without its sharp, angular points."[3] It was meant to bring together the various strands of the Reformation that disagreed sharply at significant points of doctrine.

The authors divided the catechism into 129 questions, which were themselves divided into three sections and into fifty-two "Lord's Days" to aid in the teaching endeavor. Within these divisions, the catechism discusses the major tenets of the faith, including a detailed discussion of the Apostles' Creed, the Lord's Prayer, and the Ten Commandments. To aid in the education process, the writers of the Heidelberg Catechism pioneered the system of numbering the questions of the catechism, a system that has been followed by every major catechism subsequently written.

Ursinus said that the major divisions of the catechism were the Law (the discussion of the Ten Commandments) and the gospel (the discussion of the Apostles' Creed). He explained the threefold division (the misery of man, the deliverance of man, and the thankfulness of man) of the Heidelberg Catechism by stating that the three parts actually align well with the two major divisions. The Ten Commandments (the Law) demonstrated the misery of humanity, the Apostles' Creed demonstrated the deliverance of humanity (the essence of the gospel), and prayer demonstrated the thankfulness of redeemed humanity (the response to the gospel).[4]

According to Philip Schaff, the order of the catechism corresponds to the division of the Christian life under the headings of repentance, faith, and love.[5] The second part of the catechism is the largest and contains an exposition of the entire Apostles' Creed under the divisions of God the Father, God the Son, and God the Holy Spirit.

Ursinus said that the overarching goal of the Heidelberg Catechism is to lead to salvation ("the enjoyment of the highest good") and comfort ("the assurance and confident expectation of the full and perfect enjoyment of this highest good, in the life to come, with a beginning and foretaste of it already, in this life").[6] As such, the catechism attempts to find a mediating position on several of the issues that proved contentious among Protestants. Specifically, the Heidelberg Catechism does not take a hard stance on the doctrine of election, which was then becoming a hot topic largely because of Theodore

Beza's stance on double predestination. Double predestination is the view that God has determined the eternal destiny of every human being. He has chosen some to eternal life to be saved through the work of Christ (election), and foreordained others to everlasting punishment for their sin (reprobation). Instead, the Heidelberg Catechism leaves any discussion of election or reprobation for the commentaries on the catechism, successfully rendering the catechism useful for religious groups from across the spectrum of the debates about predestination.[7] Indeed, the majority of the discussions in the Heidelberg Catechism follow this approach. The catechism does not take sides on debates regarding the order of divine decrees. The decrees of God refer to his purpose or determination with respect to all that shall come to pass. The question of the order has to do with the logical relationship between creation, predestination, and redemption established by the eternal purpose of God. There were debates which were logically prior to the others. Also, while nothing is said of the doctrine of reprobation or limited atonement (the view that God's intent in sending Christ to die on the cross was to pay for the sins and secure the redemption only of those whom God has predetermined to save, the elect), election to salvation in Christ is portrayed solely as a source of humility, gratitude, and comfort (see Questions 1, 31, 53, and 54).

However, the major dividing line of the day for Protestantism — the doctrine of the Eucharist, or the Lord's Supper — is not exactly spelled out "inclusively." Question 78 tackles the contentious issue head-on, asking, "Do then the bread and wine [of the Lord's Supper] become the very body and blood of Christ?" The catechumen is taught to respond, "Not at all: but as the water in baptism is not changed into the blood of Christ, neither is the washing away of sin itself, being only the sign and confirmation thereof appointed of God; so the bread in the Lord's Supper is not changed into the very body of Christ; though agreeably to the nature and properties of sacraments, it is called the body of Christ Jesus."

While the authors threw a bone, so to speak, to the Lutherans in their rejection of the Catholic doctrine of transubstantiation (that the bread and wine become body and blood), it is doubtful that any person with a Lutheran view of the Eucharist would be satisfied by the symbolic interpretation written in the Heidelberg Catechism.

Relevance

Within only a few years, the Heidelberg Catechism stood atop the bestseller lists of its day, supplanting even the Genevan Catechism (written by another Reformer, John Calvin). Even in the English-speaking world, the Heidelberg Catechism served the religious community as the most readily available catechism for at least a century. Because of its popularity, the Heidelberg Catechism served as the basis for several later works written in the seventeenth century, including (arguably) the one produced by the Westminster Assembly, which eventually became the most popular English catechism. Even 450 years after it was written, the Heidelberg Catechism remains an official statement of theology for most of the branches of the Reformed church worldwide today.

The fact that the Heidelberg Catechism has enjoyed such a long period of relevance demonstrates its brilliance in handling controversial issues — it focused heavily on the major issues central to the gospel and left the minor issues of the faith for personal conviction. Ursinus and his coauthors did not shy away from the difficult topics of the day, but they also did not make unnecessarily strict interpretations of Scripture. On the fundamental issues of their faith, the Heidelberg Catechism spoke clearly and without hesitation. However, at the same time, it did not promote a rigid doctrinal system and tried to establish "catholicity" (broad agreement on the fundamentals) for the newly developing Protestant faith.

Few documents in church history prove as relevant today as the Heidelberg Catechism. Two contemporary issues in particular are directly addressed by the catechism: the content of the gospel and the comfort of divine providence.

The first question of the Heidelberg Catechism provides a nutshell summary of the whole gospel:

Question 1: What is thy only comfort in life and death? Answer: That I with body and soul, both in life and death, am not my own, but belong unto my faithful Saviour Jesus Christ; who, with his precious blood, has fully satisfied for all my sins, and delivered me from all the power of the devil; and so preserves me that without the will of my heavenly Father, not a hair can fall from my head; yea, that all things must be subservient to my salvation, and therefore, by his Holy Spirit, He also assures me of eternal life, and makes me sincerely willing and ready, henceforth, to live unto him.

Rather than a stuffy static document, it "represents Christianity in its evangelical, practical, cheering aspect, not as a commanding law, not as an intellectual scheme, not as a system of outward observances, but as the best gift of God to man, as a source of peace and comfort in life and in death."[8] Indeed, while many Christians today view God's guiding hand of providence as limiting human freedom, the Heidelberg Catechism sees the doctrine as an essential element of the Christian's confident trust in God:

Question 28: What advantage is it to us to know that God has created, and by his providence does still uphold all things? Answer: That we may be patient in adversity; thankful in prosperity; and that in all things, which may hereafter befall us, we place our firm trust in our faithful God and Father, that nothing shall separate us from his love; since all creatures are so in his hand, that without his will they cannot so much as move.

The Heidelberg Catechism powerfully describes the benefits of faith in Christ:

Question 60: How are you right with God? Answer: Only by true faith in Jesus Christ. Even though my conscience accuses me of having grievously sinned against all God's commandments and of never having kept any of them, and even though I am still inclined toward all evil, nevertheless, without my deserving it at all, out of sheer grace, God grants and credits to me the perfect satisfaction, righteousness, and holiness of Christ, as if I had never sinned nor been a sinner, as if I had been as perfectly obedient as Christ was obedient for me.[9]

Schaff calls the catechism "by far the richest and deepest in Church history next to the age of Christ and his inspired apostles,"[10] and this is hardly an exaggeration. He continues, "It is the product of the heart as well as the head, full of faith and unction from above. It is fresh, lively, glowing, yet clear, sober, self-sustained. The ideas are Biblical and orthodox, and well fortified by apt Scripture proofs."[11] Even at its inception, the Heidelberg Catechism was viewed as a marvelous work of the Reformed Protestant Church. Heinrich Bullinger, Zwingli's successor and author of the Second Helvetic Confession (1566), wrote of the document, "The order of the book is clear; the matter true, good, and beautiful; the whole is luminous, fruitful, and godly; it comprehends many and great truths in a small compass. I believe that no better catechism has ever been issued."[12] For this reason, the Heidelberg Catechism is a document that deserves to be read, memorized, taught, and meditated on by every Christian of every age.

Discussion Questions

1. How would you meet Ursinus's criteria of teaching salvation ("the enjoyment of the highest good") and comfort ("the assurance and confident expectation of the full and perfect enjoyment of this highest good, in the life to come, with a beginning and foretaste of it already, in this life")?

2. How did the Heidelberg Catechism deal with the division of the 1500s? Why is there so much emphasis on the goodness of God, and how does that resolve division?

3. The Lutherans and Zwinglians fought fiercely over the Eucharist. What issues are highly divisive among Protestants today and how might we deal with them in a "Heidelberg way"? Feel free to identify either theological issues (did Jesus satisfy the wrath of God?) or more everyday ones (do we use contemporary Christian music or hymns?)

Further Reading

Bierma, Lyle D., Charles D. Gunnoe, Karin Maag, Paul W. Fields, and Zacharias Ursinus. *An Introduction to the Heidelberg Catechism: Sources, History, and Theology; With a Translation of the Smaller and Larger Catechisms of Zacharias Ursinus.* Grand Rapids, MI: Baker Academic, 2005.

de Jong, P. Y. "Calvin's Contributions to Christian Education." *Calvin Theological Journal* 2 (1967): 162–201.

———. *The Christian's ABC: Catechisms and Catechizing in England c. 1530–1740.* Oxford: Clarendon, 1996.

The Heidelberg Catechism of the Reformed Christian Religion: With Priviledge for the Benefit of the Poor. Amsterdam: printed by Henry Gartman bookseller, 1772.

Tudor, Philippa. "Religious Instruction for Children and Adolescents in the Early English Reformation." *Journal of Ecclesiastical History* 35 (1984): 391–413.

Ursinus, Zacharias. *The Commentary of Dr. Zacharias Ursinus on the Heidelberg Catechism.* Translated by G. W. Williard. Cincinnati: T. P. Bucher, 1861.

———. *The Summe of Christian Religion, Delivered by Zacharias Ursinus First, by Way of Catechism, and Then Afterwards More Enlarged by a Sound and Judicious Exposition, and Application of the Same: Wherein Also Are Debated and Resolved the Questions of Whatsoever Points of Moment Have Been, or Are Controversed in Divinitie.* Translated by David Pareus and Henry Parry. London: printed by James Young, and are to be sold by Steven Bowtell, 1645.

Ursinus, Zacharias, and Henry Parry. *The Summe of Christian Religion: Delivered in Lectures upon the Catechism [the Heidelberg Catechism].* Translated by H. Parrie. Oxford: I. Barnes, 1587.

CHAPTER 10

THIRTY-NINE ARTICLES OF RELIGION
1563

Historical Background

The Thirty-nine Articles of Religion (1563/1571) of the Church of England are hard to categorize as a creed, a confession, or a catechism. The best way to describe them might be as a short set of statements intended to set out Anglican theology as differing from the Roman Catholic Church, Protestant dissenters, Calvinists, Anabaptists, and Lutherans.[1] As the Church of England found itself in a sort of middle ground between the papacy of Rome and the Protestant Reformers, it recognized the need to set out its general beliefs. It is this need that the Thirty-nine Articles addresses.

The world that led to the establishment and adoption of the Thirty-nine Articles had, at its core, an intimate and inextricable relationship between religion and politics. When the Thirty-nine Articles were penned, state churches were emerging across Europe and religion was inextricably bound with political decisions. To understand the content of this confessional document of the fledgling Church of England, we need to explore the relationship between church and state in the sixteenth century.

Henry VIII (r. 1509–47), the king of England, inadvertently created the Anglican Church when the pope would not grant him an annulment. (Henry hoped that he could remarry to improve his chances of begetting a legitimate male heir.)[2] When he heard of the refusal, Henry cut off the Church of England from obedience to Rome and established himself (and the crown) as its supreme head.[3] But it was unclear what this Church of England was supposed to be — a miniature Catholic Church with a new leader? One of the Protestant denominations now fighting for recognition on the Continent? Over the next several years, the Church of England wrote several treatises to distinguish itself from the Catholic Church. The Ten Articles (1536), the Six Articles (1539), and the King's Book (1543) got the ball rolling in this direction.

The next few decades saw the church swing wildly in different directions. The most significant of the confessional documents came from the pen of Protestant reformer Thomas Cranmer (1489–1556), who served as Archbishop of Canterbury (the highest position in the Church of England) from 1533 until his martyrdom in 1556. Cranmer's theology was expressed in a document known as the Forty-two Articles (1552), which pushed the Church of England into what might now be called an evangelical position, distinct from Lutherans and Catholics alike. This confessional document rejected the authority of the pope, the Catholic doctrines of purgatory and transubstantiation (that the bread and wine of the Lord's Supper turn into real flesh and blood), and the celibacy of the clergy. The Forty-two Articles also denied the Lutheran view of the Eucharist and set the doctrine of justification (the action of declaring or making righteous in the sight of God) by faith as foundational for the Church of England. This monumental document was put into place by Edward VI in June of 1553. However, before the doctrines could be enforced, Edward died (a mere three weeks later), and his half sister, Mary I, was crowned queen.

Mary almost immediately moved to return the Church of England to Rome and to once again be subject to papal authority. To do so, she reestablished the Six Articles (1539) as authoritative, outlawing marriage among the clergy and reestablishing the Catholic doctrines of the Mass, confession, and the Eucharist. Mary's reign also proved to be short lived. After she used her royal power to persecute heretics — some 283 heretics (including Cranmer) were burned at the stake during her half-decade reign — Mary died unexpectedly in November 1558,[4] leaving the throne to her half sister, Elizabeth I.

Elizabeth, a devout Protestant, revived Cranmer's Forty-two Articles and returned the Church of England to the Protestant camp, an act which became official when she was excommunicated from the Roman church in 1570. Elizabeth sought true reform, and so she insisted on hosting theological debates to solidify the Anglican theological position instead of merely repeating what Cranmer had written. While the conclusions reached under Elizabeth were quite similar to Cranmer's, the new document (published in Latin in 1563) contained thirty-nine instead of forty-two articles. After a political controversy with the Lutherans, an English version of the Thirty-nine Articles was finally published in 1571.[5]

The entirety of the Elizabethan Settlement (Elizabeth's policy and, hence, also the Thirty-nine Articles) was presented as an alternative to the extremes of the day, a sort of "middle way" or *via media* between the traditional religion identified with the Roman Catholic Council of Trent and the dismissal of all church tradition as seen in the radical Protestant sects of the day such as the Anabaptists. This path on the middle ground can be seen in numerous places throughout the document, but especially in articles XIX: Of the Church; XX: Of the Authority of the Church; and XXXIV: Of the Traditions of the Church.

Content

The leaders of the Church of England under Elizabeth envisioned the Thirty-nine Articles as a document that would provide firm boundaries for the young Protestant church. The church that emerged from the Thirty-nine Articles was much closer to Cranmer's evangelical vision than it was to Catholicism, but it was also much more self-consciously traditional than Luther, Zwingli, or Calvin.

In terms of tradition, the Articles are catholic; that is, like the other Protestant confessions of the Reformation, the Articles agree with the great ecumenical councils of the church in their statements about Jesus Christ and the Trinity. They depart from the other confessions in the visible forms of their church — in their use of the prayer book and their view of church government (archbishops, bishops, priests, and deacons), for example, which closely mimic the Catholics.[6] The confession also establishes that the Roman church is indeed prone to error, like the Church of Jerusalem (among others) before it. In so doing, the Thirty-nine Articles both denies any subservience to Rome and yet acknowledges some legitimacy of the Roman church.[7] The Elizabethan Settlement also establishes the role of the national church to settle matters of the faith — denying the role traditionally held by the Church of Rome but also denying the authority given to the individual believer in many Protestant sects. Additionally, the Thirty-nine Articles provides a place for the authority of tradition. That role was not nearly as authoritative as in the Roman Catholic Church, but it was more so than in many of the radical sects of the Reformation and even than many of the Puritans desired.[8]

However, in their theology, the Articles lean much more toward the Protestant side. The Thirty-nine Articles distance themselves from Catholic teaching in confessing the sufficiency of Scripture alone to understand theological matters,[9] in condemning the "Romish Doctrine concerning Purgatory, Pardons, Worshipping and Adoration, as well of Images as of Relics, and also Invocation of Saints,"[10] and in reforming church structures by allowing services to be held in the common language of the day and in allowing clergy to marry. Moreover, "they are Protestant and evangelical in rejecting the peculiar errors and abuses of Rome, and in teaching those doctrines of Scripture and tradition, justification by faith, faith and good works, the Church, and the number of sacraments, which Luther, Zwingli, and Calvin held in common."[11] Finally, the Articles are moderately Calvinistic, in that they teach both predestination (that God predetermines who will receive salvation) and a spiritual view of the Lord's Supper as opposed to transubstantiation.

In the remainder of the strictly theological articles, the English confession clarifies the stance of the Church of England on secondary doctrinal issues, including original sin, free will, infant baptism, and the doctrines of predestination and election.[12] The stance of the Church of England on these issues serves mainly to announce to the international community her orthodoxy within mainstream Protestantism. In other words, having decisively distanced herself from Roman Catholic theology, the Church of England attempted to establish her distance from the more radical Protestant groups as well. Against the feared Anabaptists, the confession holds dogmatically and unapologetically to the practice of infant baptism and to the obedience of the believer to the magistrate.[13] The failed attempt by a group of Anabaptists to establish the kingdom of God as a political (and anarchical) society cast a large and formidable shadow over all of Protestantism in the sixteenth century.[14] Against the burgeoning rationalists, the confession suggests that, though the Bible contains everything necessary for salvation, believers should not rely so much on their own reading of Scripture that they distance themselves from the tradition and teaching of the church.[15]

The Articles are also the most Erastian of the confessions, which means that they affirm the superiority of the state over the church. Remember that the reason the Anglicans came into being at all was to be an official church that would serve the will of the king. The Anglicans themselves soon took on a life of their own, using the separation from Rome as the chance to introduce real reform into the English church, but their alliance with the state remained an important part of their identity.

Legacy

The Thirty-nine Articles were a useful statement of faith for a young church attempting to carve out its own place among the other emerging Protestants of the Reformation. The document itself proved far more valuable than perhaps even its most ardent supporters could have imagined. Under its umbrella, opposing groups such as the official English representatives at the Calvinist Synod of Dort[16] and the firmly Arminian Archbishop of Canterbury, William Laud (1573–1645), could coexist without needing to amend the document. In fact, famous church historian and sometime Bishop of Salisbury, Gilbert Burnet, writing more than a century after the adoption of the Thirty-nine Articles, comments on the varied interpretations of the Thirty-nine Articles already present in the Church of England. In the nineteenth century, John Henry Newman, a prominent Anglican writer who later converted to Catholicism, could even use the positive attitude of the Thirty-nine Articles to demonstrate his own appreciation of the Roman Catholic Church.[17] The document was narrow enough to identify the Church of England as a unique expression of Christendom found in the British Isles, but wide enough to allow all English Protestants to find comfort in it. Even in the twenty-first century, the Church of England encompasses a wide variety of doctrinal camps — all of which still subscribe (at least officially) to the Thirty-nine Articles.

One of the most common points of controversy — both soon after the Elizabethan Settlement and today — focuses on the document's stance on the doctrines of predestination and election. The modern discussion often overlooks the historical context of the confession, failing to note that at this point in history, practically all Protestants were dogmatic about doctrines. However, in perhaps the most telling discussion of the doctrine of predestination, the Thirty-nine Articles warns that this doctrine can provide comfort for believers and can be of real damage for unbelievers. Thus, the church officially urges caution when handling this doctrine, a warning that has hardly been heeded.[18]

Relevance

The middle ground established by the Thirty-nine Articles and the rest of the documents of the Elizabethan Settlement provides guidelines for navigating the potentially rough waters of religious polemics. By providing room to disagree within a broad range of orthodoxy, the Thirty-nine Articles created a fertile ground for theological exploration while simultaneously identifying the potential pitfalls of heresy. Additionally, unbeknownst to the founders of the Elizabethan Settlement, Anglicanism would soon move well beyond the British Isles. Within a century and a half, the Anglican Church spread to the North American colonies, and, during the eighteenth, nineteenth, and twentieth centuries, the Anglican Church expanded to the rest of the continents, bringing with it the theological foundation established by the Thirty-nine Articles.

Perhaps the most relevant section of the Thirty-nine Articles for today's church is the brilliant and vivid rebuke of those who continually dispute the minutia of predestination and election. It would be wonderful if more Reformed Christians talked about God's sovereign grace in this manner:

> As the godly consideration of Predestination, and our Election in Christ, is full of sweet, pleasant, and unspeakable comfort to godly persons, and such as feel in themselves the working of the Spirit of Christ, mortifying the works of the flesh, and their earthly members, and drawing up their mind to high and heavenly things, as well because it doth greatly establish and confirm their faith of eternal Salvation to be enjoyed through Christ, as because it doth fervently kindle their love towards God: So,

for curious and carnal persons, lacking the Spirit of Christ, to have continually before their eyes the sentence of God's Predestination, is a most dangerous downfall, whereby the Devil doth thrust them either into desperation, or into wretchlessness of most unclean living, no less perilous than desperation.

Put most simply, God's electing grace turns us to the cross of Christ, not only to the divine decree of election itself.

Discussion Questions

1. What do you think of a confession that is based on finding a middle road? What are the positives and negatives of that approach?
2. Given that Anglicanism is one of the most theologically diverse groups of Christians, have the Thirty-nine Articles succeeded or failed? Is it better to have a broad or a narrow confession?
3. What is the ideal balance in your view between Scripture and the traditions of the church (either of a particular church or going back to earliest times)? Do you think that it's valuable to acknowledge Christian tradition? Why or why not?
4. Why do you think that the Anglicans wanted to distance themselves from the radical Protestants?

Further Reading

Burnet, Gilbert. *An Exposition of the Thirty-nine Articles of the Church of England.* London: Printed by R. Roberts, for Ri. Chiswell, at the Rose and Crown in St. Paul's Church-Yard, 1699.

MacCulloch, Diarmaid. *Thomas Cranmer: A Life.* New Haven, CT; London: Yale Univ. Press, 1996.

Newman, John Henry. *Remarks on Certain Passages in the Thirty-nine Articles.* London, 1841.

CHAPTER 11

WESTMINSTER CONFESSION OF FAITH

1646

Historical Background

The Thirty-nine Articles satisfied the Protestants in England for some time, but in a few generations conflict broke out again. The more radical Protestants, called Puritans, preferred to use the Bible alone, to have very simple worship services and live modestly, without bishops, rituals, or any hints of Catholicism. As Anglicanism became a sign of the upper class and Puritanism a sign of the middle class, the country entered civil war in 1642. By the following decade, the Puritans had won control of the government, but Catholics and Arminians (who advocated free will and a universal invitation to salvation) hovered in the wings in hopes of recovering the throne. To guard against the influence of Catholic king James I and Arminian Archbishop William Laud, Parliament convened a council of 121 theologians (along with thirty laymen, six Scottish commissioners, and nine Scottish elders) in 1646 and charged the assembly with overseeing a "more perfect reformation of the Church."[1]

The Westminster Confession of Faith (WCF) is a Reformed confession produced by that Westminster Assembly in London. Intended to set the doctrinal standards for the Church of England, it became a powerful force in the Church of Scotland and has influenced Presbyterian churches all over the world. Centuries later, numerous churches and denominations worldwide look to the Westminster Confession as their standard of doctrine, subordinate, of course, to Scripture.

Initially, Parliament charged the assembly with the task of revising the Thirty-nine Articles (1563), the doctrinal statement that had served as the official stance of the Church of England since the early days of Elizabeth I's reign. However, when the English Parliament forged a political alliance with their Scottish counterparts, the assembly aborted this endeavor in favor of more thorough reforms in favor of Protestantism.[2] When Anglican troops regained the government and reestablished the monarchy, the Puritan groups kept the Westminster Confession (especially in Scotland) and carried it with them on their missionary expeditions, while the English government returned to the Thirty-nine Articles for its own use.

Content

The Westminster Assembly initially met to settle what you might call "housekeeping" issues — how churches were to be organized, how wrongdoers were to be disciplined, and what qualified a person for the clergy.[3] Remember that at this time the Puritans had complete control of England, so they were thinking about how to build a society based on their ideals rather than explaining what they believed about God. However, rival groups were still competing for power. The assembly eventually decided that its main purpose was to connect Christian doctrine to society, particularly a Calvinist brand of Christianity (one that believes that God predetermines who will be saved). Although the confession itself saw little official use, it met its goal to bring systematic Calvinism to everyday life; part of its appeal was that it was broad enough to include multiple kinds of Calvinists but also intent on practical Christian living in light of Calvinist doctrine. (Not only are suggestions along this line found in the confession, but the assembly also produced a Larger and Shorter catechism.)[4]

To combat an anti-predestination view (predestination is the idea that God predetermines who will be saved), the assembly allowed their own predestinarian theology to permeate their official documents. In fact, of the thirty-three chapters in the Confession of Faith, at least fourteen could be said to be laid firmly on the foundation of predestination.

Against the Arminians of the day, the assembly made sure to include the five classical points of Calvinism (TULIP — Total depravity,[5] Unconditional election,[6] Limited atonement,[7] Irresistible grace,[8] and the Perseverance of the saints[9]) in the document. So people are said to be unable to will their own conversion. (Remember the earlier chapter, on the Council of Orange? God has to awaken in the human heart the desire to be reconciled to himself.) Since people can't save themselves, God has to save them, and he does so without considering their good works, heritage, or any other condition. Christ died to save those God chose, those whom in his mercy God was pleased to rescue from this state of being spiritually dead. The grace of God overcomes all resistance to him and all sin that prevents union with God. Finally, since God alone has to initiate salvation, he is also responsible for seeing it through to the end, and those that he brings into the Christian fold, he keeps there.

In addition to the doctrine of predestination as it relates to salvation, the Confession of Faith also included the accompanying doctrine of reprobation, teaching that God not only elects some to salvation but that the others he "foreordain[s] to everlasting death."[10] This sentiment is repeated in Article VII: "He extendeth or withholdeth mercy as He pleaseth, for the glory of His sovereign power of

His creatures, to pass by, and to ordain them to dishonor and wrath for their sin, to the praise of His glorious justice." The members of the assembly wrote these articles deliberately because they wanted to preserve the doctrine of God's sovereign power (that is, the belief that God is in control of everything, including who is or is not saved) against the Arminian position that seemed to limit it (since God's desire for everyone to be saved is, in the Arminian view, dependent on people's response to him).

However, the confession qualified this predestinarian theology with a discussion upholding human free will[11] and the necessity of repentance in the life of the believer,[12] all the while maintaining a view of salvation that emphasized divine grace. What the reader should take away from the doctrine of predestination is an appreciation of the mercy of God (rather than speculating on how election works or priding themselves on being part of the "in" group).

While the issue of predestination is a significant topic in the Confession of Faith, the confession was more than merely a discussion of predestination. The documents produced by the assembly actually covered the breadth of Christian theology. The Confession of Faith includes chapters on broadly orthodox theology — the doctrine of God, his essence, and divine character, good works, marriage and divorce, and synods[13] and church councils, among others. Notably, according to John Frame, Benjamin Warfield called the opening chapter on the doctrine of Scripture "the best single chapter in any Protestant confession."[14] God's covenants with his people are emphasized (chapter 7), and "[i]ts doctrine of redemption structured according to God's acts (chapters 10 – 13) and human response (chapters 14 – 17)."[15]

In other words, this confession served as far more than a discussion of a single doctrinal issue. The assembly saw theology as an all-encompassing endeavor with the right teaching of biblical truth affecting every aspect of life.

The other major contribution that the document makes to Calvinist believers is in its explanations of the sacraments and church order. Against both Lutherans and Catholics, the confession holds to a largely spiritual version of the Lord's Supper, stating that the bread and wine are not merely symbols or literal flesh and blood but are a gateway to actual contact with God: "The body and blood of Christ being then not corporally or carnally in, with or under the bread and wine [the first part takes aim at the Catholics, the latter part at the Lutherans, and the next part at the Zwinglians, who believe only in symbolism], but spiritually, present to the faith of believers in that ordinance, as the elements themselves are to the outward senses." Similarly, the confession outlines Calvinist stances on baptism, the Sabbath, and the role of the laypeople and the secular government in church matters, all of which varied among the Protestant denominations in England at that time. The goal of the assembly was to make Calvinist Christianity a workable system for the nation, and that meant considering matters that veer from the strictly theological (like appropriate activities on the Sabbath).

Although the confession is heavily Calvinist, its appeal lies just as much in its ability to bring high theology to the everyday believer. For instance, consider its practical statement on the authority of Scripture, which opens the confession:

> VII. All things in Scripture are not alike plain in themselves, nor alike clear unto all: yet those things which are necessary to be known, believed, and observed for salvation are so clearly propounded, and opened in some place of Scripture or other, that not only the learned, but the unlearned, in a due use of the ordinary means, may attain unto a sufficient understanding of them … IX. The infallible rule of interpretation of Scripture is the Scripture itself: and therefore, when there is a question about the true and full sense of any Scripture (which is not manifold, but one), it must be searched and known by other places that speak more clearly.

In other words, the assembly acknowledged that the Bible can be a hard book to read (and that merely surface-level readings are not always the right ones; the Bible is not Wikipedia), but also argues that the parts that are really necessary to understand salvation can be understood by an ordinary person. It also mentions that since all the books of the Bible are inspired by the Holy Spirit, the reader can find answers in one section that illuminate puzzling parts of another. The section also lists the books in the Bible as well as the reason that the church accepts certain books and rejects others. Other examples range from the Trinity, the Chalcedonian depiction of Christ (fully human and fully divine), the three stages of salvation (justification, sanctification, and glorification),[16] and the way that God uses natural as well as supernatural events to work his will. While these answers are far from exhaustive, the confession is expert at making quick, pointed statements that capture the heart of the matter at hand.

Because of its blend of high theology, pastoral matters, and social life, the confession proved a hit with Christians of many denominations. Ironically, the Westminster Confession of Faith had far more impact outside of the Church of England than within it. The works of the assembly not only became official statements of the Scottish Church but also served as the basis for the foundational theological statements of two other English sects and, through them, several other denominations. The Westminster Confession of Faith also made its way across the Atlantic, forming the basis of the statement of faith of the Philadelphia Association of Baptists as well as the early Presbyterians in the colonies. The document still officially serves some of these sects several hundred years later.

The Westminster Confession of Faith can hardly be boiled down to a single issue. The Westminster Assembly surely saw themselves as doing more than simply repeating a theological system by rote recall. They were engaged in practical matters of extreme import, including the implications of a robust theology on everyday life — such as how to trust in God and how much weight to give the supernatural in major events.

Relevance

One of the most remarkable aspects of the Westminster Assembly is how a group of theologians labored amid extreme political turmoil to follow a higher calling. The temptation in any political crisis is to support one's own side or to avoid offending anyone at all. There may be a little evidence of the first temptation in the more extreme statements on predestination, but as a whole the document is virtually free from it. It certainly takes a firm stance, but hardly a vindictive one. Rather, the overall theme of the confession is in understanding how far-reaching the implications of seemingly academic doctrines can be. The Westminster Assembly clearly understood that practice follows teaching, and for the assembly, the theology of the church could not be divorced from the actions of the laity. The confession puts its heart into making the implications of this theology understandable rather than repeating a set of ideas.

Aside from continuing to serve as the theological foundation of several denominations, the all-encompassing nature of this version of Reformed theology stands as perhaps the most enduring aspect of the Confession of Faith and the supporting documents published by the assembly. The Westminster Standards left practically no aspect of church life (or human life, for that matter) untouched. The biblical and theological thinking that undergirds this system simply cannot be reduced to a single doctrine, as is often tried in much contemporary theological discussion. Specifically, the Westminster Confession does not limit its discussion of predestinarian theology merely to a discussion of salvation, nor does it focus on small portions of Scripture to prove its stance. The attempt to strike some balance between human free will — albeit one corrupted by depravity — and divine sovereignty demonstrates well this desire to incorporate the whole testimony of Scripture.[17]

Those who find the Thirty-nine Articles too general and noncommittal and the Book of Concord too Lutheran may be drawn to the Westminster Confession of Faith as an alternative reading of Scripture that falls within the bounds of orthodox theology.

The assembly's focus on divine prerogative and gracious activity, highlighted especially by the centrality of the covenant of grace, has often led to this version of Reformed theology being referred to as "the doctrines of grace."[18] The fine-tuned nature of the confession, due largely to the amount of time taken to craft the document as well as to the large number of theologians involved in the process, has allowed it (and its daughter confessions) to stand the test of time. Ultimately, the Westminster Assembly succeeded in coordinating its theology within the historically accepted creeds and confessions, separating themselves from the heterodox theologies promulgated throughout Europe and even readily found in the British Isles.

Besides setting an example for modern theologians, the confession will also help believers broaden their thinking. One of the more jarring aspects of the document is its discussions of everyday life — regulating the Sabbath, for example, which is hardly something that churches spend much time discussing nowadays.[19] The fact is that the confession does open up its readers to seeing Christian life in a more all-encompassing way. Additionally, the confession gives excellent summaries of the decisions of the major early councils and their importance for Christian life. (The same thing that I am trying to do in this book!) While the language of the seventeenth century may intimidate some readers, the sections are relatively short and worth the effort to understand God's providence and the serious implications of living a Christian life.

The confession overflows with scriptural proofs, and it is anything but a cranky "hammerheaded" Calvinism. Because the document is Calvinistic, its tone is that of a theology permeated by divine grace. The confession is thoroughly concerned with maintaining conversation with the great creeds of the church that elaborated a robust doctrine of the Trinity (Nicaea) and Christ's nature (Chalcedon). For all of these reasons, the Westminster Confession remains relevant as one of the most significant statements of faith for the Protestant tradition.

Discussion Questions

1. If a person disagrees with the Westminster Assembly on major points of doctrine (for example, that God predetermines whether a person goes to heaven), how can he or she benefit from the Confession of Faith?
2. What do you make of the fact that this confession was written during a civil war? Does it lead you to suspect it of being exclusive or vindictive?
3. Besides being a confession for Calvinists, the Westminster Confession of Faith was meant to be a confession for a nation. What do you make of this? Would a national confession be appropriate today? Why or why not?

Further Reading

Andrewes, Lancelot. *Two Answers to Cardinal Perrron [Sic] and Two Speeches in the Star Chamber.* Londini: excudebat Felix Kynston pro RB and Andraea Hebb, 1629.

Boersma, Hans. *A Hot Pepper Corn: Richard Baxter's Doctrine of Justification in Its Seventeenth-Century Context of Controversy.* Zoetermeer, Netherlands: Boekencentrum, 1993.

Duffy, E. *The Stripping of the Altars: Traditional Religion in England, 1400–1580.* New Haven, CT; London: Yale Univ. Press, 1992.

MacCulloch, Diarmaid. *Thomas Cranmer: A Life.* New Haven, CT; London: Yale Univ. Press, 1996.

McCullough, Peter E. *Sermons at Court: Politics and Religion in Elizabethan and Jacobean Preaching.* Cambridge: Cambridge Univ. Press, 1998.

Packer, J. I. *The Redemption and Restoration of Man in the Thought of Richard Baxter: A Study in Puritan Theology.* Carlisle: Paternoster, 2003.

Tyacke, Nicholas. *Anti-Calvinists: The Rise of English Arminianism c. 1590–1640*. Oxford: Clarendon, 1987.

Weir, David A. *The Origins of the Federal Theology in Sixteenth-Century Reformation Thought*. Oxford: Clarendon, 1989.

CHAPTER 12

SECOND VATICAN COUNCIL

1962–65

Historical Background

The Second Vatican Council (known as Vatican II), which met from 1962 to 1965, is incredibly significant for the Roman Catholic Church, as the time when the church's monumental modern developments took effect. Called by Pope John XXIII, with observers from other denominations present, the Second Vatican Council represented an *aggiornamento* (a "bringing up to date") for the Roman Catholic Church. The *aggiornamento* had been a hundred years in the making, when events in the nineteenth century had set in motion the final collapse of Christendom. Faced with a Europe that was increasingly skeptical of Catholic influence (political and otherwise), the church prepared to critically examine itself in order to revitalize its witness.

During the nineteenth century, the church was rocked by the rising tide of political revolution in Europe and the increasing popularity of liberal theology, which denied central teachings of the early creeds, and historical criticism, which sought to separate within the

Bible a "historical Jesus" from a supposed "mythological Jesus." Its political influence waned with the loss of the Papal States to the Italian resurgence (*risorgimento*) in 1871. The pope was allowed to maintain control of the Vatican, but everything else was taken from him. Pius IX refused to leave the Vatican; a self-imposed exile and protest.

During this time, Pius IX reasserted his authority by calling for a general church council, to be held at the Vatican (Vatican I, 1870) — the first sanctioned council of the Catholic Church since Trent. Two major matters were at issue: papal infallibility (whether the pope's statements on theology could never be wrong, provided they were made officially) and the universal jurisdiction of the pope (thus overriding the authority of individual bishops), each of which increased the pope's authority. With the significant exception of Leo XIII (who was influential in developing a modern approach to social justice in the newly industrialized world), the popes that followed issued strict bans on modernist thinking. Any attempts at reconciling Catholic teaching with modern historical criticism or at combining traditional medieval thinking with modern philosophy and theology were condemned.

But there were also signs that changes were taking place in the thinking of Catholic theologians. One sign was a resurgence of the study of the early church fathers, which led theologians to question whether certain Catholic practices were universal in the church's history. It also led to a renewed interest in liturgical practices. The struggle with the church's relation to modern culture and these renewal movements set the stage for Vatican II.

The Calling of a New Council: John XXIII and Vatican II

The historical background is important because "if Vatican II needs to be understood as a repudiation of certain aspects of the nineteenth century and an embracing of certain others, it also must be understood as a response to the immediate and profound changes taking place in the world at mid-century."[1]

The rise of communism and the fall of the Iron Curtain, the dawn of the atomic age, a world devastated by the second world war in a forty-year period, and the rise of democracy all marked the middle of the twentieth century. The United States, "the only industrial nation to survive World War II with its cities, factories, and roads intact, the largely Protestant democracy mocked by European bishops at Vatican I, now dominated the world."[2] The Vatican of the nineteenth century had rejected freedom of speech, press, and religion, but now these values were being promoted by the United States as the best hope to defeat communism. Many were wondering if the Roman Catholic Church could change from its nineteenth-century responses to address twentieth-century realities.

In 1958, John XXIII was elected as pope. He was not the first choice to replace Pius XII; no candidate was able to gain the majority. So the cardinals agreed to a compromise candidate who they assumed would be in office only for a few years. He was elected pope on the twelfth ballot, and chose a name, John, that had not been used by a pope since the fifteenth century.

In spite of the fact that he was seen as merely a caretaker pope, John made it clear that he would be no such thing. Just three months into his pontificate, John announced that he planned to call a churchwide council. This announcement was surprising for several reasons. For the first time in history, a council was being called when there were no major doctrinal issues or crises that needed to be solved. He told no one of his plans, not even his advisors, who were as shocked as everyone else. His announcement took place on January 25, which is the close of the traditional week of prayer for Christian unity. In his announcement he made it clear that other Christian denominations would be welcomed to come to the council as observers in a way that had never been done before. There were schemata for Vatican II. It was not entirely an open agenda, making it possible for John to invite the bishops to submit their opinions on what the council should discuss. Nearly two thousand bishops responded with suggestions.

The goals that John XXIII expressed in calling for the council were symbolized in three ideas: *aggiornamento* (updating), *ressourcement* (return to sources), and development of doctrine. The concept of *aggiornamento* was not about updating doctrine but about communicating these doctrines to the modern world. "The church's teaching remained, but its understanding and formulation had to be changed, as John XXIII would often say."[3]

Ressourcement was about the return of the language and pastoral emphasis that were present in Scripture and the patristic fathers. "It entails a return to the sources with a view not to confirming the present but to making changes in it to conform it to a more authentic or more appropriate past ... a more profound tradition."[4] This return to the sources played a large role in the changes that were made to the Catholic liturgy. It was about how tradition was to be understood and what weight the ancient traditions had for the church of the twentieth-century.

Development of doctrine was a more controversial concept. American theologian John Courtney Murray described it as the "issue under all issues" at Vatican II.[5] This was evidenced in the council's treatment of several issues, none larger than Murray's specialty: the separation of church and state. Previously, the concept of separation of church and state had been condemned, but now the bishops agreed that this was a legitimate doctrine of the church, based on the idea of a "living," rather than static, tradition. Vatican II was not about doctrine as much as it was about tradition. It was about self-understanding, the nature of the church, and the expression of the Catholic Church to the modern world.

The Reforms of Vatican II

Vatican II officially began on October 11, 1962, with John XXIII setting the tone for the council with his opening address, *Gaudet Mater*

Ecclesia ("Mother Church Rejoices"). John wanted the texts of the council to be expressed in positive terms instead of condemnations and canons.

The first session of the council addressed two main issues: the liturgy and the doctrine of revelation. With regard to the former, the bishops of the council determined that Latin should be retained for the Catholic Mass, with concessions being made to the vernacular — the common languages of everyday Catholics. This ruling gave local bishops the authority to use whatever language would best serve their church members and showed that the church was attempting to be relevant and keep up with post–World War II globalization. However, wholesale vernacularization of the Latin liturgy came in a later reform. In the years following the council, the liturgy rapidly shifted from Latin entirely to common languages.

In addition, the importance of Scripture in the liturgy was highlighted by a lectionary that was to be read during services. The council made it clear that one of their principal concerns "was to restore the proclamation and study of the word of God to its central place in the life of the church."[6] Along with this came a renewed emphasis on the homily, or sermon, and on preaching that emphasized the texts found in the lectionary each Sunday.

The first session of Vatican II also made strides in the doctrine of revelation. Although continuing the idea of a two-source theory of revelation that had been outlined at Trent (that is, both Scripture and Christian tradition are authoritative for church teaching, since tradition represents what has been said through the Holy Spirit), the Vatican documents approached the matter in a new way. Revelation is a matter of encountering God — hence, Jesus himself was revelation. The council adopted the idea that Christ is the revelation, the Word of the Father, and that revelation flows from him in two streams, Scripture and tradition. The documents presented Scripture and tradition less as the two places where revelation can be found than as the two tools that believers use for revelation. "This sacred tradition, therefore, and Sacred Scripture of both the Old and New Testaments are like a mirror in which the pilgrim Church on earth looks at God, from whom she has received everything, until she is brought finally to see Him as He is, face to face."[7] The new definition lost nothing of Catholic dogma but came across as friendlier to those unfamiliar with the tradition.

John XXIII died shortly after the end of the first session of Vatican II and was replaced by Paul VI (1963–78). In many ways, Paul was very different from John, but one thing the two men shared was agreement about the goals of Vatican II. Paul made it clear that the council would continue as John had envisioned.

The second and third sessions of Vatican II focused on the structure and hierarchy of the church as well as its relationship to secular culture.

One major issue that was discussed was the nature of the bishop. Whereas bishops had long been treated as the hands and feet of the pope, doing what he commanded, the council decided that in order to follow the pattern of the early church, bishops should have more authority in their own regions. They were given the freedom to make authoritative decisions on their own in order to determine what was best for the people they served. Furthermore, a document on the church, known as *Lumen Gentium*, emphasized that the clergy and laity together constitute one "people of God." The document contains a high Mariology (view of Mary, Jesus' mother), while at the same time affirming the unique mediatorship of Christ: "In the words of the apostle there is but one mediator … (1 Tim. 2:5–6). But Mary's function as mother of humankind in no way obscures or diminishes this unique mediation of Christ, but rather shows its power."[8]

The council also addressed the relationship of the church to non-Christian religions, declaring that open dialogue with other religions was encouraged. While the old Roman Catholic principle stated *extra ecclesiam non salus est* ("there is no salvation outside the [Catholic] Church"), the council focused on the positive aspects in other religions: for instance, the council stated in regard to Eastern faiths, "the Catholic Church rejects nothing of what is true and holy in these religions."[9] Vatican II affirmed that the Catholic Church is the church of Christ and the universal sacrament of salvation, and that what is holy and good in other religions are those elements *shared* with the Catholic Church. Because other religions have elements of truth, beauty, and goodness (and sometimes worship one God), the church recognized that they express truths or partial truths about God that the church itself affirms; however, the council still held to the fact that Christ is the way, the truth, and the life (John 14:6). The council also addressed the political issue of religious liberty, affirming that other religions are free to practice as they saw fit. Other religions are free to practice not because they are true but because their practitioners have human dignity and freedom from coercion.

The new statement on divine revelation, *Dei Verbum*, was put forth during the third session of the council. The emphasis of the new document was on the fullness of God's revelation in Jesus Christ, carried on by Scripture and tradition (a "one-source" view of revelation). The text also insisted that the laity should read and study the Bible and that the Bible should be translated into native languages.

Finally, the document *Gaudium et Spes* ("Pastoral Constitution on the Church in the Modern World") honored Leo's earlier legacy of social justice. It included the church's teaching on human rights, dignity, and social justice, and addressed contemporary issues like world peace and economics. The church was rejecting the stance of the nineteenth century and coming to see itself as a helper for all people.

Relevance

Some saw Vatican II as a complete break from the past, an utterly new beginning, which in itself would pose a problem for a genuinely Catholic theology, whereas others saw it as a new emphasis in unity with all that came before it, and to be interpreted in the light of church history and dogma.

Not everyone was pleased with the outcome of Vatican II, and not everything that was put on paper was easy to carry out. However, the efforts of the Catholic Church to become more involved in the lives of the laity and to interact with other religions was generally appreciated. Some, however, saw Vatican II as the beginning of the decline of the Catholic Church. They believed that all of the changes led to a crisis of authority.

Even though Vatican II signaled the formal end of the Catholic reaction against Protestantism known as the Counter-Reformation, Protestant and Catholic disagreement still continues. Dialogue between Catholics and Protestants began almost immediately after Vatican II and continues today, yet there has been little real progress other than the Joint Declaration on the Decree of Justification that was signed by the Vatican and the Lutheran World Federation (1999), which clarified differences and fostered goodwill. Pope John Paul II made it a goal of his pontificate finally to heal the Great Schism, the division between Roman Catholicism and Eastern Orthodoxy that has existed since AD 1054, but that goal has proven elusive.

Non-Catholics can glean wisdom from some of the formulations of the Second Vatican Council. Perhaps most important, they can learn from the council's urging for Christians to be the church in the world in a relevant and faithful way.

Discussion Questions

1. How do you think the Catholic Church changed at Vatican II? Do you see these changes as big changes? Why or why not?
2. Do you think that the changes at Vatican II were good or bad for the Catholic Church? Why?
3. Of all the changes, which one surprises you the most?
4. Do you think doctrinal expressions need to be updated? Do you see a danger in updating doctrine?

5. Recognizing that the church lives in history and culture, how do you think the church should adapt to changes in culture and history? What do you think is not changeable?

Further Reading

Alberigo, Giuseppe. *A Brief History of Vatican II*. Translated by Matthew Sherry. Maryknoll, NY: Orbis, 2006.

Gaillardetz, Richard R., and Catherine E. Clifford. *Keys to the Council: Unlocking the Teaching of Vatican II*. Collegeville, MN: Liturgical Press, 2012.

Kelly, Joseph F. *The Ecumenical Councils of the Catholic Church: A History*. Collegeville, MN: Liturgical Press, 2009.

O'Malley, John W. *What Happened at Vatican II*. Cambridge: Belknap Press, 2008.

CHAPTER 13

MODERN CONFESSIONS

LAUSANNE COVENANT AND CHICAGO STATEMENT ON BIBLICAL INERRANCY

1974 and 1978

Introduction

Christian doctrine did not stop developing after the ancient councils. Although the majority of new confessions of faith came about during the Reformation in order to distinguish Christian bodies from one another and to affirm the historic ecumenical councils, more recent times have seen joint confessions from Christians of all kinds of denominations. Indeed, a new series of movements are calling themselves ecumenical to show that they are attempting to reestablish the unity that has been eroded by the splintering sectarianism of modern Christianity. Just as new dilemmas had prompted the ancient Christians to define their beliefs more sharply, the fresh challenges presented by a well-connected, technologically advanced world have led Christians of all stripes to seek doctrinal unity to address the challenges posed by the modern world.

Two of these challenges include biblical criticism and world evangelism. The late nineteenth century saw the rise of a skeptical academic class that claimed hitherto unknown techniques for unlocking the origins of the Bible. With the Bible being treated more and more like a merely human book, as prone to mistakes as any other human book, various conservative Protestant churches found it necessary to define and defend the inerrancy, or complete accuracy, of Scripture. As a result, the Chicago Statement on Biblical Inerrancy was drafted in 1978 by a gathering of several hundred evangelical church leaders.

Although historical-critical readings of Scripture that focus primarily and almost exclusively on the human origins of a text had been attempted in both the early and medieval church, the results had never before seemed both so plausible and so threatening to the faith. The Chicago statement addressed this new challenge by incorporating the historical-critical techniques when appropriate, defining what was inappropriate, and expounding a definition of sacred Scripture that was consistent with that of the historic church. While the Chicago statement clarified what the church has traditionally believed about the Bible, it specifically addressed an issue that the early church never really had to consider. In that regard, it serves as an example of a modern confession.

The problem of world evangelism dealt less with doctrinal matters than it did with the reality of the challenges of globalization. Population explosions, advances in communication, and the number of new worldviews that were suddenly on the front doorstep of the West demanded a way forward for Christian missions. The Lausanne Conference, in 1974, was a careful reexamination of the past for both its successes and its mistakes, with the hopes of producing a faithful witness for Christ in the years to come.

The new councils[1] differed from the old ecumenical councils in one important detail, however; they did not consider themselves authoritative. Wary of the abuses of church authority in the past, the councils self-consciously advised their hearers to use their decisions for guidance only, not as dogma.

Chicago Statement on Biblical Inerrancy (1978)

Historical Background

As early as AD 170, a list of canonical books, or books believed by the church to be part of the Bible, set forth a basic explanation of the inspiration and inerrancy of the Bible. After explaining the traditions behind each human author and the authority with which each author wrote, the list adds a curious note on the problem of contradictions: "And so, though various elements may be taught in the individual books of the Gospels, nevertheless this makes no difference to the faith of believers, since by the one sovereign Spirit all things have been declared."[2]

Far from being a reaction to modern scholars who questioned the authority of the Bible, the idea of divine inspiration of Scripture and its reliability was a staple of early Christian belief. It was accepted that the authors wrote in their own human capacity,[3] and that the Bible was not a miracle in and of itself; nevertheless, it was equally true that God stood behind the authors and guided them in their writing to accomplish his ends. J. N. D. Kelly cites Irenaeus, Gregory of Nyssa, Theodore of Mopsuestia, Origen, and Gregory of Nazianzus as holding to the inspiration (and therefore, the reliability and truthfulness) of Holy Scripture down to the smallest detail of its content. Indeed, he says, "This attitude was fairly widespread, and although some of the fathers elaborated it more than others, their general view was that Scripture was not only exempt from error but contained nothing that was superfluous."[4]

While there have been opponents of inerrancy throughout church history, the most substantial challenge came from the Enlightenment — commonly referred to as the Age of Reason — according to which anything that could not be verified through rational argumentation and evidence must be rejected as irrational. The prevailing attitude was a sort of reductionism.[5] The skeptics agreed that the Bible was a human book, but why take it as anything more than a human book? By the same token, why treat the apparent contradictions between the individual books as anything other than contradictions, on the dubious presumption that God had intended to write seemingly opposite statements? The doctrine of divine inspiration seemed to be special pleading. Similar logic led to a denial of the miracles and resurrection of Christ, on the grounds that when any other historical sources speak of such events, the reader knows to take them as legends.

In response to this skepticism, some Christians reinterpreted the Bible according to "modern" criteria. Known as theological modernists, they employed higher criticism, a methodology that sought to identify the literary origins of the biblical text and treated it as a merely human collection of documents. Veering into the equal and opposite error, some extreme fundamentalists[6] overemphasized the Bible's divine origin and rendered its human part as irrelevant. The Chicago statement, which emerged from the fundamentalist wing, wanted to strike a balance that retained the divine inspiration and inerrancy of Scripture while at the same time taking into account its genuinely human features.

Therefore, more than two hundred evangelical leaders met in the fall of 1978 at a conference sponsored by the International Council on Biblical Inerrancy and drafted the Chicago Statement on Biblical Inerrancy (CSBI). As an indication of the scope of the conference, the list includes leaders in a variety of disciplines, such as history, cultural criticism, biblical studies, evangelism, philosophy, and systematic theology.

Content

Theologian Millard Erickson explains inerrancy as follows: "Inerrancy is the doctrine that the Bible is fully truthful in all of its teachings."[7] When all the relevant facts are known, and when properly interpreted, Scripture never contradicts itself, nor does it misrepresent the facts. The phrase "when all the relevant facts are known" is key to understanding the Chicago statement, which affirmed that God's hand lies behind Scripture but also was concerned that the hyperdivine interpretation sometimes led to misinterpretation by neglecting to take into account qualities such as genre, language, indirect reports, and so forth.

The CSBI is composed of a short statement of five points,[8] a section of nineteen articles that describe the major positions that academics held on Scripture along with the opinion of the council on which ones were to be affirmed and which were to be denied, and an exposition of the doctrine of inerrancy in relation to the other teachings of Scripture. Among the most important points are the following:

First, Scripture's authority comes from its being the Word of God, not from the church or tradition, and is thereby authoritative and binding. Since this teaching forms the foundation for everything else that follows, it is worth quoting the words of the council at length:

> The Church's part was to discern the canon that God had created, not to devise one of its own. The word *canon*, signifying a rule or standard, is a pointer to authority, which means the right to rule and control. Authority in Christianity belongs to God in His revelation, which means, on the one hand, Jesus Christ, the living Word, and, on the other hand, Holy Scripture, the written Word. But the authority of Christ and that of Scripture are one. As our Prophet, Christ testified that Scripture cannot be broken. As our Priest and King, He devoted His earthly life to fulfilling the law and the prophets, even dying in obedience to the words

of Messianic prophecy. Thus, as He saw Scripture attesting Him and His authority, so by His own submission to Scripture He attested its authority. As He bowed to His Father's instruction given in His Bible (our Old Testament), so He requires His disciples to do — not, however, in isolation but in conjunction with the apostolic witness to Himself that He undertook to inspire by His gift of the Holy Spirit.[9]

Second, against the objection that human language is too limited to convey a divine message, the council stated that God could and did use human language for his message to humanity, particularly since he had made humankind in his image.

Third, while God's inspiration did not eliminate human authorship and literary style, it did guarantee that their utterances were true and trustworthy. This point struck back at the hyperdivine interpretation by acknowledging that "[h]istory must be treated as history, poetry as poetry, hyperbole and metaphor as hyperbole and metaphor, generalization and approximation as what they are, and so forth. Differences between literary conventions in Bible times and in ours must also be observed."[10]

Fourth, only the autographs (the original copies) of Scripture were inerrant, but this does not render the doctrine irrelevant today since an accurate representation of the original writings of Scripture can be constructed from the thousands of historical Scripture manuscripts we have. On a related note, the council was careful to acknowledge the limitations of translation work while also being optimistic about the quality of modern Bibles: "No translation is or can be perfect, and all translations are an additional step away from the autograph. Yet the verdict of linguistic science is that English-speaking Christians, at least, are exceedingly well served in these days with a host of excellent translations and have no cause for hesitating to conclude that the true Word of God is within their reach."[11]

Fifth, while inerrancy and infallibility can be distinguished, they cannot be separated; that is, the Bible cannot be at the same time infallible and errant in its assertions. The council defined "infallible" as "not deliberately misleading or having been misled" and "inerrant" as "not mistaken, free from error."

Sixth, inerrancy is rooted in the doctrine of inspiration. That is, the dependability of the Bible, like the dependability of our salvation, can be found only in the character of God. Because God is wholly perfect, it would be mistaken to conclude that his very word could be anything other than inerrant.

Seventh, while affirming that inerrancy is not necessary for salvation, it is vital to the Christian faith, and its rejection leads to serious consequences in the individual and the church.

The document concludes by stating that the Bible is a gift of God to make the reader "wise unto salvation," and expresses its concern at what would happen if its importance were lost.

Relevance

Questions about the Bible are abundant in our day, and modern Christian churches are often fuzzy on issues such as the canon (list of books in the Bible), the relationship between Paul's teaching and that of Jesus, and the reliability of the original text and its transmission (how it was passed down through history). Inspiration and inerrancy are also vital, as many Christian doctrines are available for human knowledge only through divine revelation. The Bible is one of the ways, along with the illumination of the Holy Spirit, that we "see through a glass, darkly." It is crucial to know whether we are really seeing through the glass at all.

The CSBI answers some of these questions but also challenges those who ask to consider whether they are more influenced by real problems with the text or prevailing tendencies in the culture: "We are concerned at that casual, inadvertent and seemingly thoughtless way in which a belief of such far-reaching importance has been given up by so many in our day."[12] Doubt regarding the divine origin of the Bible often comes less from careful study than the general mood of the culture. Like every other theological assertion, scriptural inerrancy deserves careful consideration, as well as a willingness to search out and challenge the presumptions that have merely seeped into our minds.

One of the other reasons that the Chicago Statement on Biblical Inerrancy is so important is that it walks the fine line between theological liberalism on the one hand and fundamentalism on the other. While liberalism so analyses and assesses the background and literary features of the Bible (that is to say the *human* features of the Bible) that the text's divine authenticity is diminished, fundamentalism so emphasizes the Holy Spirit's role in the writing of the Scriptures (that is to say the *divine* features of the Bible), that the text is in no way the product of human authorship. Liberals deny inerrancy because of the parts of the Bible that seem purely a product of a distant time and the multitude of textual variants in the New Testament manuscripts,[13] while fundamentalists assert that only one version of the text (quite often the King James Version) contains the inspired words of God. Both positions fail to do justice to the dual authorship of Scripture, asserted by the CSBI. The modest position of the CSBI assures that the Holy Spirit was indeed present in inspiring the text of Scripture, thereby ensuring its factual accuracy while still allowing for the human elements of different styles in the writing process and inevitable errors that occur in textual transmission — the copying and preserving of biblical manuscripts.

While it acknowledges that it ought not to be given creedal status, the CSBI offers a balanced, thought-provoking answer to the question of the Bible as divine revelation. The CSBI reasserts the classical understanding of inerrancy, not as a constructed doctrine to be foisted upon the text of Scripture but as a result of the reliability and trustworthy character of God and an idea expressly approved by Jesus Christ.

The Lausanne Covenant (1974)

Historical Background

The Lausanne Covenant was drafted by the International Congress on World Evangelization in Lausanne, Switzerland, in 1974 as an agreement about the meaning of the gospel and how it was to be spread throughout the world. The covenant, used here in the sense of "a binding contract" or "a very solemn personal commitment,"[14] was signed by 2,300 representatives from more than 150 nations of all branches of the Christian church.

The covenant was made possible by ecumenical efforts from earlier in the twentieth century, particularly the World Missions Conference (WMC) in Edinburgh in 1910, but the price of that ecumenism had been steep. To achieve their goal of gathering denominations with seemingly irreconcilable differences, the organizers of the Edinburgh conference had refused to define the content of the gospel or to make doctrine the underlying basis for agreement. Although the conference took the important step of creating the International Missionary Council (IMC), two world wars and the creep of theological liberalism, which downplayed differences between religions and the doctrine that Jesus was both God and human and the savior of sinful humanity, sapped energy and resources from Western churches' evangelistic efforts. When a later generation attempted to correct this neglect by integrating the IMC into the World Council of Churches (WCC) as its missionary wing, it only led to redefining evangelism in terms of social justice alone. As a result, the Edinburgh conference not only failed to achieve a truly ecumenical approach to missions but saw all of its work co-opted by a single faction, the rising liberal wing.

The Lausanne Conference was an attempt to continue the ecumenical dialogue that Edinburgh had begun while nudging evangelism toward a more balanced definition that included witness to salvation through Christ as well as social justice. It also represented a necessary adjustment to a world that had grown much smaller with new abilities in communication and transportation. (And keep in mind that this is well before the internet!) Historic Christendom was now rubbing shoulders with all sorts of new philosophies and religions, while Christian demographics were shifting rapidly to the Global South (Asia, Africa, and Latin America). There was a sense that the conference was taking place on the cusp of a tremendous global change, and that the church needed to make itself ready.

Content

The members of the conference adhered to a five-point definition of evangelicalism that was set out by Billy Graham, a major international preacher and the driving force behind the conference. The definition included "(1) the authority of Scripture as the 'infallible Word of God'; (2) the 'lostness of man' outside of Christ; (3) that salvation is of Christ alone; (4) witness to Christ is through both word and deed; (5) that evangelism of the lost is completely necessary."[15]

If the conference was evangelical, however, it was also far from reactionary and demonstrated careful consideration of the excesses of both left and right. Additionally, despite the agreement of the participants on the five points, the conference still represented parties with significant differences who had agreed to put those differences aside. In his opening address, Georges-Andre Chevallaz summed up the ecumenism of the gathering in this way: "We have also the certainty, that clinging to its essence, its purity, its simplicity of teaching, its concern for the welfare of others, its awareness of the relativity of human concepts, Christianity goes beyond ideological quarrels, interests, and partisan loyalties." In other words, Lausanne's focus on the shared core of the faith could unite Christians across ideological boundaries for the sake of cooperation in evangelism.[16]

The covenant begins with an affirmation of the Trinity and of the sovereignty and supremacy of God. It acknowledges the inspiration, trustworthiness, authority, and infallibility of the Bible and that Scripture is the instrument of the Holy Spirit for the conversion of humanity.[17] The covenant emphasizes the deep need for evangelism, pointing out that there were 2.7 billion people, more than two-thirds of humanity at the time of the covenant, who had never heard the gospel of Christ, and acknowledges that the number of unevangelized "is a standing rebuke to us and to the whole Church."[18] But what is evangelism supposed to look like? John Stott highlighted the heraldic character of evangelism as opposed to its results: "To evangelize is to spread the good news that Jesus Christ died for our sins and was raised from the dead according to the Scriptures, and that as the reigning Lord he now offers the forgiveness of sins and the liberating gifts of the Spirit to all who repent and believe."[19] Thus, Lausanne deliberately makes a distinction between evangelism and conversion, and recognizes that although Christians bear responsibility to witness to Jesus Christ in the world, conversion is the work of the Holy Spirit.[20]

On the other hand, just as the covenant makes it clear that it desires both conversion and evangelism but that it is wrong to confuse the two, it also states that it desires both social justice and evangelism, but that they are different responsibilities in the Christian life. Against some liberal theologians, the covenant states that "reconciliation with other people is not reconciliation with God," that social justice and evangelism are not the same thing, and that "political liberation" is not salvation. To equate these actions with salvation is actually to secularize the gospel, which is inherently supernatural. The Christian's true battle is with "principalities and powers of evil," which can be fought only with the "spiritual weapons of truth and prayer."[21] However, the conference affirmed that Christian presence in political affairs is necessary as a matter of obedience to Christ and that the message of salvation entails the denunciation of all forms of evil and injustice.[22] As such, the conference wanted to avoid the opposite error that evangelism can replace social responsibility; both are areas that Christians are called to carry out.

The leaders of the conference also emphasized evangelism as opposed to interfaith dialogue. While interfaith dialogue has a purpose in evangelical Christianity, the leaders of the conference worried that it could lead to syncretism, or the tendency to blend appealing beliefs in different religions, rather than proclaiming the truth that God has given. On this point, John Stott added that although dialogue with other faiths is important, the kind of dialogue that Scripture commends is respectful listening and understanding in the effort to persuade others to come to Christ. Evangelism does not have to mean refusing to interact with other points of view, but it does mean that Christians are to put their trust in what God has said about himself rather than putting their trust in their own ability to search for truth.

While the covenant rejects syncretism on the one hand, on the other it affirms that the expression of the one gospel differs from culture to culture. The conference praises God's "many-colored wisdom" and rejects cultural imperialism and the idea that the gospel can be adequately expressed only by a single culture. It urges Christians to approach evangelism in a way that is consistent with the dignity of each culture. As opposed to the practice of some European missionaries in the past, the covenant also encourages the growth of locally attuned training programs for both laity and clergy.[23]

In short, the conference distanced itself from traditional evangelism that had identified Christianity too closely with Europe while also keeping away from the new, pluralistic Christianity that was all too willing to challenge social injustice but reluctant to challenge other worldviews or sin. The balance was an approach that emphasized proclaiming the message of Christ, even at personal cost (this position was sharpened later, in the Manila Manifesto) but also reminded Christians of their place in society and their place in a global, as opposed to European-led, church.

Relevance

Lausanne is relevant primarily because it defines the role of evangelism so clearly. Evangelism, as Lausanne indicates, means proclaiming the good news of Jesus Christ and inviting others to enter into a relationship with him. As Lausanne further specifies, the task of evangelism is different from the results of evangelism; the church's task is to be faithful in evangelism. Although apologetics, theology, and social action are all legitimate and important activities of the church, none are capable of persuading those outside the church to enter into relationship with Christ. That is the work of the Holy Spirit, without whom no one can have saving faith in Christ (1 Cor. 12:3).[24] Evangelism is likewise distinguishable from social action, and Lausanne points out that confusing those two activities of the church is a kind of secularization. For believers of this generation, these distinctions can help remind us of our duties, our purpose, and the message of God on the matter.

Lausanne is also helpful for calling attention to the corporate character of evangelism. Evangelism is a task of the church as a whole rather than of heroic individuals within it, even though some are more especially gifted in the task of evangelism than others. The whole church by virtue of baptism is called into the mission of God to redeem sinners and reconcile all of creation to himself (Matt. 28:19; John 3). The covenant condemns the "ghettoization" of evangelicalism within safe enclaves and advocates costly discipleship in those arenas where Christians are largely unwelcome and are subject to persecution.[25] It issues a call to Christians to live simply for the sake of the gospel, reminding its readers that the church exists not to preserve itself but rather to welcome the lost into its fellowship.

Lausanne is also relevant for its insistence that doctrine is essential for cooperation in the task of world evangelization. Earlier World Missions Conferences failed in their objectives in large part because they refused to define the meaning of the gospel or to define the criteria by which success in evangelism should be judged. By returning to the fundamentals of the faith — the Trinity, the authority of Scripture, the centrality, uniqueness, and necessity of Jesus Christ for salvation, and the purposes of God in history and at the end of history — Lausanne encourages the contemporary church to be rooted in Scripture and insists, against many trends, that sound doctrine is the basis of sound evangelism.

Finally, the Lausanne Missions Conference has spawned the Lausanne Movement, an ongoing cooperative effort among participants committed to the covenant to continue the process of reflection on the meaning of the covenant in light of changed circumstances.[26] It has also produced the Lausanne Theology Working Group, which has issued a number of statements in light of the commitments of Lausanne. The most important documents to emerge from the Lausanne Movement are the Manila Manifesto (1989) and the Capetown Declaration (2010), which are both extensions and elucidations of the core affirmations of Lausanne.

Discussion Questions

1. How does the Chicago statement help us to interpret the problem of apparent contradictions in the Bible? Give an example.
2. Faced with a rationalist objection (for example, "Why should I consider the Bible to be more than merely human?"), how would you respond?
3. What is the role of evangelism in the West? Have most people heard the gospel and simply rejected it? If so, what is the appropriate way to witness as a Christian?
4. How would you engage in respectful dialogue with nonbelievers that is also evangelistic? Is that a contradiction in terms?
5. What other major issue do you think should have an ecumenical conference today?

Further Reading

"The Chicago Statement on Biblical Inerrancy," *http://www.spurgeon .org/~phil/creeds/chicago.htm*.

Geisler, Norman L., ed. *Inerrancy*. Grand Rapids, MI: Zondervan, 1980.

Holcomb, Justin S., ed. *Christian Theologies of Scripture: A Comparative Introduction*. New York: New York Univ. Press, 2006.

"Lausanne Movement," *http://www.lausanne.org/en/*.

Stott, John R. W., ed. *Making Christ Known: Historic Mission Documents from the Lausanne Movement, 1974–1989*. Grand Rapids, MI: Eerdmans, 1997.

CONCLUSION

Dogma can in no way limit a limitless God ... For me, dogma is only a gateway to contemplation and is an instrument of freedom and not of restriction. It preserves mystery for the human mind. Dogma is the guardian of mystery. Doctrines are spiritually significant in ways we cannot fathom.

— Flannery O'Connor, *The Habit of Being*

What are we to make of the role of a human church in creating written documents about God? Are we better off relying on the sense that we ourselves can make of the Bible or the experiences that we have? My position (as you have probably figured out) is that even the finer points of Christian theology come out in our worship and lives. The humanity and deity of Jesus, the Trinity, the trust that we know we can put in Scripture are all beside us in our services on Sunday morning and impact the way we honor God in our daily lives. And if that's the case, then we ought to tackle high theology the same way that we tackle sin and the needs of the Christian community — as a body of Christ, using the parts of the body that are best suited to the task. The statements that are introduced here are the fruit of parts of the body that God gathered to proclaim and explain his gospel, stretching nearly two thousand years into the past.

In Paul's second letter to the church at Corinth (2 Cor. 9:13–15), he speaks to the church of two activities that follow God's gracious and abundant lovingkindness: material generosity and confession of the gospel.[27] According to John Webster, "Both acts are echoes of what Paul calls (v. 14) 'the surpassing grace of God in you'; both, that is, are brought into being by the limitless lavishness of God which Paul celebrates in the climactic words of the chapter: 'Thanks be to God for his inexpressible gift' (v. 15)."[28] What this means, for Webster, is that the act of confession, before a document, is a basic act of the church. As he puts it, "Before it is proposition or oath of allegiance, the confession of the church is a cry of acknowledgement of the unstoppable miracle of God's mercy."[29]

At its basic level, "Confession . . . is that event in which the speech of the church is arrested, grasped and transfigured by the self-giving presence of God. To confess is to cry out in acknowledgement of the sheer gratuity of what the gospel declares, that in and as the man Jesus, in the power of the Holy Spirit, God's glory is the glory of his self-giving, his radiant generosity."[30]

Understanding that the theological statements in this book[31] are specific instances of the Christian act of confession is significant because it helps us remember that confessions are not primarily about doctrine and theology; they are ultimately about worship. Lest we think that fine points of doctrine and the minutiae of theological debate are merely intellectual exercises, the fact that confession is about praise helps ground the way that we use confessional documents.

John Webster looks at the way creeds and confessions function in church life and argues that they "properly emerge out of one of the primary defining activities of the church, the *act of confession*."[32] In the very act of confession, says Webster, "the church binds itself to the gospel."[33] It "is the act of astonished, fearful and grateful acknowledgement that the gospel is the one word by which to live and die; in making its confession, the church lifts up its voice to do what it *must* do — speak with amazement of the goodness and truth of the gospel and the gospel's God."[34] Webster's point is to help us remember that confession is a central and primary act of the church's life and that the creeds and confessions exist only secondarily as documents that are particular instances of the act of confession.

Additionally, learning about creeds, confessions, catechisms, and councils is important so that we do not repeat the mistakes of the past or exhibit our natural tendency for, as C. S. Lewis dubs it, "chronological snobbery." As Lewis points out,

> Every age has its own outlook. It is specially good at seeing certain truths and specially liable to make certain mistakes. We all, therefore, need the books that will correct the characteristic mistakes of our own period. And that means the old books.... We may be sure that the characteristic blindness of the twentieth century — the blindness about which posterity will ask, 'But how *could* they have thought that?' — lies where we have never suspected it.... None of us can fully escape this blindness, but we shall certainly increase it, and weaken our guard against it, if we read only modern books.... The only palliative is to keep the clean sea breeze of the centuries blowing through our minds, and this can be done only by reading old books. Not, of course, that there is any magic about the past. People were no cleverer then than they are now; they made as many mistakes as we. But not the *same* mistakes.[35]

Learning how Christians throughout history have wrestled with the tough questions of our faith gives us a valuable perspective that deepens our understanding of the Christian faith, increases our dependence on God's revelation in Jesus Christ and Holy Scriptures, fuels our worship of God, increases our love for each other, and motivates mission to the world.

NOTES

Introduction

1. J. N. D. Kelly, *Early Christian Creeds*, 3rd ed. (New York: Continuum, 1972), 1.

2. R. P. Martin, "Creed," in *New Bible Dictionary*, ed. D. R. W. Wood et al. (Leicester, England; Downers Grove, IL: InterVarsity, 1996). Martin writes, "There are clear indications that what appear as creedal fragments, set in the context of the church's missionary preaching, cultic worship and defense against paganism, are already detectable in the NT" (241).

3. Bruce Demarest, "Heresy," in *New Dictionary of Theology*, ed. Sinclair B. Ferguson, David F. Wright, and J. I. Packer (Downers Grove, IL: IVP Academic, 1988), 293.

4. Irenaeus, *Against Heresies* 3.4.1 – 2.

5. Demarest, "Heresy," 292.

6. John Webster, "Confession and Confessions," in *Confessing God: Essays in Christian Dogmatics II* (London: T&T Clark, 2005), 76.

7. Where the reader sees "confessions" in brackets, Lewis originally used "creeds." His intention was a denominational statement of faith rather than a general orthodox one, however, and I have made the change here to avoid confusion. C. S. Lewis, *Mere Christianity* (New York: HarperCollins, 2009), xv.

8. Cyril of Jerusalem, *Prochatechesis* 11.

9. Tom Nettles, "An Encouragement to Use Catechisms," *Founders Journal* 10 (Fall 1992), *http://www.founders.org/journal/fj10/article3.html*, accessed December 4, 2013.

10. John Nordling, "The Catechism: The Heart of the Reformation," *Logia* 16, no. 4 (2007): 5 – 13.

11. Johann M. Reu, *Dr. Martin Luther's Small Catechism: A History of Its Origin, Its Distribution and Its Use* (Chicago: Wartburg, 1929), 13.

12. In one of his letters, he wrote, "Believe me, Monseigneur, the Church of God will never preserve itself without a Catechism, for it is like the seed to keep the good grain from dying out, and causing it to multiply from age to age. And therefore, if you desire to build an edifice which shall be of long duration, and which shall not soon fall into decay, make provision for the children being

instructed in a good Catechism, which may shew them briefly, and in language level to their tender age, wherein true Christianity consists. This Catechism will serve two purposes, to wit, as an introduction to the whole people, so that every one may profit from what shall be preached, and also to enable them to discern when any presumptuous person puts forward strange doctrine." John Calvin, "To the Protector Somerset," *Selected Works of John Calvin: Tracts and Letters*, vol. 5 (Letters, Part 2 1545–53), ed. Henry Beveridge and Jules Bonnet (Banner of Truth, 2009), letter 229.

13. Arnold, "Early Church Catechesis," 46–51.

14. Nordling, "The Catechism," 8.

15. Ibid., 9.

16. Webster, "Confession and Confessions," 73–74.

17. Nicaea I (325), Constantinople I (381), Ephesus (431), Chalcedon (451), Constantinople II (553), Constantinople III (681), and Nicaea II (787). The first seven councils of the church are referred to as ecumenical councils because they are, at least in principle, accepted by the Catholics, Protestants, and Orthodox as authoritative in some way or another.

18. Constantinople IV (870), Lateran I (1123), Lateran II (1139), Lateran III (1179), Lateran IV (1215), Lyon I (1245), Lyon II (1274), Vienne (1312), Constance (1414–18), Basel, Ferrara and Florence (1431–45), Lateran V (1512–17), Trent (1545–63), Vatican I (1870), and Vatican II (1962–65).

19. Some scholars suggest the conference in Galatians 2:1–10 is referring to the Jerusalem Council, while others think it was an earlier meeting that Paul and Barnabas had with James, Peter, and John.

Chapter 1: Apostles' Creed

1. Pope Siricius is the first to use the term Apostles' Creed (*symbolum apostolorum*) to describe this creed in his letter to the Council of Milan in ca. 390.

2. The creed technically contains more than twelve articles, but it is customary to retain the twelvefold structure to retain the apostolic symbolism. The legend that each apostle contributed one article goes back at least to the fifth century with Rufinus of Aquiliea, but the claim is in wider circulation in the sixth century. It was common among medieval theologians. See Rufinus, *Commentary on the Apostles' Creed* 2, *http://www.newadvent.org/fathers/2711.htm*, accessed April 25, 2013; Pseudo-Augustine, Migne, *Patrologia Latina* (=PL), XXXIX 2189; and Prudentius, Migne, *PL* LxxXIX 1034. Henri de Lubac indicates that one can divide the creed into statements about God himself and statements about Christ's humanity and ministry on earth, and each of these parts can be further subdivided into seven articles, yielding a total of fourteen articles.

Such was the approach of the great medieval scholastic theologians Alexander of Hales, Bonaventure, and Thomas Aquinas. Henri de Lubac, *The Christian Faith: The Structure of the Apostles' Creed*, trans. Illtyd Trethowan and John Saward (London: Geoffrey Chapman, 1986), 20.

3. Henri de Lubac writes, "In the second century people spoke as a matter of course about a 'rule of faith,' a 'rule of truth,' an 'immutable rule,' and there was a justifiable conviction that this rule went back to the apostles."

4. Although the text of the Old Roman Creed cannot be reproduced satisfactorily because of the many variants, the Apostles' Creed seems to have added the phrases "Maker of heaven and earth"; "descended into hell"; "the communion of saints"; "life everlasting"; and the words "conceived"; "suffered"; "died"; and "Catholic." See J. N. D. Kelly, *Early Christian Creeds*, 3rd ed. (New York: Continuum, 1972), 377–78.

5. Philip Schaff, *The Creeds of Christendom: With a History and Critical Notes*, 6th ed., vol. 1 (New York: Harper and Brothers, 1919), 14.

6. Kelly, *Early Christian Creeds*, 368.

7. A rather complex discussion of various levels of hell developed around this belief (notably with purgatory as a kind of "antechamber" to hell), which are elaborately extended and exposited in Dante's *Divine Comedy*. The doctrine emerges from a reading of 1 Peter 3:18–20 and 4:6, and Revelation 20:11–15, and noncanonical Christian literature such as *Odes of Solomon* 17:9–12; 22:1, 42, and especially *The Gospel of Nicodemus*, which contains an elaborate account of the harrowing of hell. This belief had some currency among the early fathers of the church, but its popularity was much more extensive in the medieval period, when it was dramatized extensively. See, for example, Karl Tamburr, *The Harrowing of Hell in Medieval England* (Woodbridge, UK: Boydell and Brewer, 2007).

8. See, for example, Robert Jenson and Carl Braaten, eds., *Sin, Death, and the Devil* (Grand Rapids, MI: Eerdmans, 2000).

9. Frederick J. Murphy, *Early Judaism: The Exile to the Time of Christ* (Grand Rapids, MI: Baker, 1996), 184. Sheol is mentioned copiously in the Old Testament, and there is an interesting account of a soul returning from sheol in 1 Samuel 28:3–25, in which Saul asks the Witch of Endor to conjure Samuel's shade.

10. Berard Marthaler, *The Creed: The Apostolic Faith in Contemporary Theology*, 3rd rev. ed. (New London, CT: Twenty-Third Publications, 2007), 171.

11. This was Calvin's position in *Institutes of the Christian Tradition*. See 2.16.8ff. It is interesting to note that contemporary Catholic theology is trending in this direction as well. See, for example, Hans Urs von Balthasar, *Dare We Hope That All Men May Be Saved? With a Short Discourse on Hell* (San Francisco: Ignatius, 1988); Hans Urs von Balthasar, *Mysterium Paschale* (San Francisco: Ignatius, 2000).

12. Ignatius, *Epistle to the Smyrneans* 8, *http://www.newadvent.org/fathers/0109 .htm*, accessed May 5, 2013.

13. Cited in J. W. Strawson, *The Epistles of St. Ignatius*, 97, *http://www .earlychristianwritings.com/srawley/smyrnaeans.html*, accessed May 4, 2013.

14. C. S. Lewis, *The Weight of Glory* (New York: HarperCollins, 2009), 46.

Chapter 2: Council of Nicaea and the Nicene Creed

1. "The common views passed on to us of the Roman emperor's gathering all the bishops of every city to sit in council together are astonishing. These Christian leaders were the survivors of horrific persecution. When groups of Christians were tortured or tossed to the lions for entertainment in coliseums, some survived and would be released again. We can imagine these bishops arrived limping, some with lost limbs, burns, and deep scars. It was reported that when Constantine greeted Paphnutios, a bishop from the Thebaid in the Nile Valley whose eye had been gouged out during the persecution, he reverently kissed the empty socket. The bishops traveled at the emperor's expense, and his guests were treated sumptuously while in attendance at the council. Bishops were becoming civic and political figures, and within the space of a few decades they were even players in the affairs of state." Robert Louis Wilken, *The First Thousand Years* (New Haven: Yale Univ. Press, 2012), 91. When you read this, remember that Roman involvement in Christianity is a big deal — all of these bishops carried in their memory some picture of what Roman authority looked like — not a single Christian leader was without an image of a friend or loved-one martyred. And now Roman authority, in this man Constantine, was turning to help the church. Constantine gathered these bishops to solve a problem.

2. Rowan Williams, *Arius: Heresy and Tradition*, rev. ed. (Grand Rapids, MI: Eerdmans, 2001), 98.

3. Origen, *On First Principles* 1.1.6.

4. Origen explained this by a theory of "eternal generation" of the Son by the Father. *On First Principles* 1.2.4.

5. The original creed of Nicaea 325 finishes this paragraph as follows: "came down and became incarnate, becoming man, suffered and rose again on the third day, ascended to the heavens, will come to judge the living and the dead."

6. The original creed of Nicaea 325 ends at this point, and appends anathemas against Arius: "But as for those who say, 'There was when He was not,' and 'Before being born He was not,' and that He came into existence out of nothing, or who assert that the Son of God is of a different hypostasis or substance, or is subject to alteration or change — these the Catholic and apostolic Church

anathematizes." J. N. D. Kelly, *Early Christian Creeds*, 3rd ed. (New York: Continuum, 1972), 215–16.

7. "And the Son" — or *filioque* in Latin — appears in written editions in the late eighth century, but was apparently common to the usage of the creed much earlier and is fully consistent with the Trinitarian theology of Augustine of Hippo, who regularly taught double procession. Kelly, *Early Christian Creeds*, 301, 358ff. Its addition, whenever it occurred, was made without any consultation with the Greek churches, and contributed greatly to the later schism between Catholic and Orthodox churches.

8. "Again, when the Bishops said that the Word must be described as the True Power and Image of the Father, in all things exact and like the Father, and as unalterable, and as always, and as in Him without division (for never was the Word not, but He was always, existing everlastingly with the Father, as the radiance of light), Eusebius and his fellows endured indeed, as not daring to contradict, being put to shame by the arguments which were urged against them; but withal they were caught whispering to each other and winking with their eyes, that 'like,' and 'always,' and 'power,' and 'in Him,' were, as before, common to us and the Son, and that it was no difficulty to agree to these … but since the generation of the Son from the Father is not according to the nature of men, and not only like, but also inseparable from the essence of the Father, and He and the Father are one, as He has said Himself, and the Word is ever in the Father and the Father in the Word, as the radiance stands towards the light (for this the phrase itself indicates), therefore the Council, as understanding this, suitably wrote 'one in essence,' that they might both defeat the perverseness of the heretics, and shew that the Word was other than originated things." Athanasius, *Defense of the Nicene Symbol* 20.

Chapter 3: Councils of Ephesus

1. J. N. D. Kelly, *Early Christian Doctrines*, rev. ed. (Peabody, MA: Prince Press, 2004), 310.

2. Once they learned of Nestorius's intentions, the Arians themselves set it ablaze. John McGuckin, *St. Cyril of Alexandria and the Christological Controversy* (Crestwood, NY: St. Vladimir's Seminary Press, 2004), 24.

3. Ibid.

4. Ibid., 37.

5. Ibid., 33.

6. Henry Chadwick, "The Christological Debate I: To the First Council of Ephesus (431)," in *The Church in Ancient Society: From Galilee to Gregory the Great* (Oxford: Oxford Univ. Press, 2001), 12.

7. Ibid., 13. According to Chadwick, the Roman government passed a law limiting the number of monks in Alexandria to six hundred and ordered them not to interfere any longer in secular affairs.

8. A good summary of the two views, as well as an example of how Antiochene and Alexandrian interpretations clashed at Ephesus, can be found in Donald Fairbairn, "Grace and the Central Issue of the Christological Controversy," in *Grace and Christology in the Early Church* (Oxford: Oxford Univ. Press, 2003).

9. Nestorius, *The Bazaar of Heracleides*, trans. G. R. Driver and Leonard Hodgson (Oxford: Clarendon, 1925), 9. Nestorius wrote *The Bazaar of Heracleides* after the Council at Ephesus in a vain attempt to clear his name. In the book, Nestorius lists a number of heresies that he wishes to refute, including Apollinarism (the idea that Jesus did not have a human mind), but Arianism and Manichaeanism appear most often, and he accuses Cyril of being "compelled to join either the Arians or Manichaeans in such as way as to admit either than he suffered not naturally any one of these things or only in illusion and in fiction" (39).

10. Nestorius, *Bazaar of Heracleides*, 58.

11. Ibid., 73.

12. McGuckin, *St. Cyril of Alexandria*, 130.

13. Nestorius, *Bazaar of Heracleides*, 47, "Thou wilt confess aloud with us that there are not two Gods the Words or two Sons or two only begottens, but one, and so on with all the rest of them."

14. Cyril of Alexandria, *Five Tomes against Nestorius* (Oxford: James Parker and Co., 1881), 70.

15. Ibid., 77.

16. Ibid., 97.

17. Kelly, *Early Christian Doctrines*, 311.

18. Ibid., 324.

19. McGuckin, *St. Cyril of Alexandria*, 47.

20. Ibid., 64.

21. Ibid., 60.

22. For the text of a Nestorian monument in China, see "East Asian History Sourcebook: Ch'ing-Tsing: Nestorian Tablet: Eulogizing the Propagation of the Illustrious Religion in China, with a Preface, composed by a priest of the Syriac Church, 781 A.D." *http://www.fordham.edu/halsall/eastasia/781nestorian.asp.*

23. Kevin Vanhoozer, "Righting the Wrongs of the Reformation," Wheaton Theology Conference, 2010.

Chapter 4: Council of Chalcedon

1. Justo L. Gonzalez, *The Story of Christianity*, vol. 1 (San Francisco: HarperSan-Francisco, 1984), 252.

2. J. N. D. Kelly, *Early Christian Doctrines*, rev. ed. (Peabody, MA: Prince Press, 2004), 339.

3. Thomas Bokenkotter, *A Concise History of the Catholic Church* (New York: Image Books, 1977, 2004), 90.

4. Gonzalez, *Story of Christianity*, 256. The three councils are Nicaea (325), Constantinople (381), and Ephesus (431).

5. Henry Bettenson and Christ Maunder, eds., *Documents of the Christian Church*, 3rd ed. (Oxford: Oxford Univ. Press, 1999), 56.

6. George A. Lindbeck, *The Nature of Doctrine: Religion and Theology in a Post-liberal Age* (Louisville: Westminster John Knox Press, 1984, 2009).

7. Gonzalez, *Story of Christianity*, 257.

8. See Max Lucado, "It Began in a Manger," *http://maxlucado.com/read/topical /it-began-in-a-manger-christmas/*, accessed September 13, 2013.

9. B. B. Warfield, "The 'Two Natures' and Recent Christological Speculation," in *The Person and Work of Christ*, ed. Samuel G. Craig (Philadelphia: P&R Publishing, 1950), 211–62.

Chapter 5: Athanasian Creed

1. T. F. Torrance, *The Trinitarian Faith* (Edinburgh: T&T Clark, 1995), 117ff. John Behr, *The Nicene Faith*, vol. 2 (Crestwood, NY: St. Vladimir's Seminary Press, 2004), 163ff.

2. A recent edition of *On the Incarnation* even has an introduction written by C. S. Lewis. Available in many editions now, the introduction by Lewis has become itself a known work for its remarkable encouragement and charge to "read old books" for the benefit of Christian development. That is, to escape the tyranny of the contemporary moment and all of its tacit presuppositions and paradigms.

3. Philip Schaff, *The Creeds of Christendom: With a History and Critical Notes*, 6th ed., vol. 1 (New York: Harper and Brothers, 1919), 36.

4. J. N. D. Kelly, *The Athanasian Creed* (New York: Harper and Row, 1964), 1.

5. Quoted in Robert L. Wilken, "Introducing the Athanasian Creed," *Currents in Theology and Mission* 6, no. 1 (Fall 1979): 5.

6. For example: "... *haec tria Christianae confessionis principia*." Epistola 136, *Sancti Anselmi Opera Omnia*, ed. F. S. Schmitt (Edinburgh: Thomas Nelson and Sons, 1946–61), vol. 3, 280. This was noted by Jasper Hopkins and Herbert

Richardson in their review of J. N. D. Kelly's book *Early Christian Doctrines* (*Harvard Theological Review* 60, no. 4 [October 1967]: 483).

7. Schaff, *Creeds of Christendom*, vol. 1, 40. However, it must also be noted that this creed never achieved ecumenical status or formal ecclesial sanction, as the Greek church rejected its assertion of the double procession of the Spirit (what is known as the *filioque*).

8. Ibid., 41.

9. *"Nous avuouns les trois symboles: savoir: des Apôtres, de Nicée, et d'Athanase, parce qu'ils sont conformes a la parole de Dieu," Gallic Confession of 1559,* Article 5. Liberal Protestant attempts to separate Calvin from the confessions and suggest he held them in low regard have been misguided, although Calvin is always careful to hold the Word of God itself on a higher strata than any creed or confession. Stephen M. Reynolds, "Calvin's View of the Athanasian and Nicene Creeds," *Westminster Theological Journal* 23, no. 1 (November 1960): 33.

10. Philip Schaff, *History of the Christian Church*, vol. 3 (New York: Charles Scribner's Sons, 1910), 524. Full quote: "This Creed is unsurpassed as a masterpiece of logical clearness, rigor, and precision; and so far as it is possible at all to state in limited dialectic form, and to protect against heresy, the inexhaustible depths of a mystery of faith into which the angels desire to look, this liturgical theological confession achieves the task."

11. Also known as the *filioque* controversy: does the Holy Spirit come only from the Father, or both the Father and the Son?

12. Philip Schaff, *The Creeds of Christendom: With a History and Critical Notes*, vol. 2 (New York: Harper and Brothers, 1919), 66–71.

13. The creed itself names no heresies nor singles out any particular heretics by name for damnation or exile. This is actually pretty unique in ancient Christian creeds. However, the creed makes use of the language of "person" in a way that allows it to skirt between Sabellianism on the one hand and tritheism on the other. And it maintains orthodox Christology by stating that Christ has a rational soul (against Apollinarianism), and sets forth the relationship between the human and divine natures of Christ in such a way as to avoid Nestorianism, Eutychianism, and Monophysitism.

14. *"Aequalis gloria, coaeterna maiestas."*

15. The creed claims that "whatever is predicated of God *substantialiter* (i.e., of God as substance or essence) can properly be predicated of the three persons severally, since each is the divine essence." Kelly, *Athanasian Creed*, 83. This can be found in Augustine, *On the Trinity* 8.1: "For example, the Father is God, the Son is God, the Holy Spirit is God; and the Father is good, the Son is good, the Holy Spirit is good; and the Father is omnipotent, the Son is omnipotent, the Holy Spirit is omnipotent: yet there are not three Gods, nor three good, nor

three omnipotent, but one Who is God, good, omnipotent, the Trinity itself." It seems likely that the author of *Quincunque* had this work at his disposal.

16. The chief theological advocate was Eunomius of Cyzicus, whose arguments were dismantled by Basil of Caesarea in his works *Against Eunomius* and *On the Holy Spirit*. R. P. C. Hanson, *The Search for the Christian Doctrine of God* (Edinburgh: T&T Clark, 1988), 679ff.

17. The opponent of the creed feared that the orthodox were drifting toward an earlier heresy, monarchianism, which stated that the unity of the universe demonstrated that there could be only one mind behind it. One of the arguments for dating *Quincunque* in the early to mid-fifth century is the emerging contest between the rapidly eroding Roman Empire and the Vandals. The Vandals were Christians, but were full advocates of the Arian doctrine of a generated Son. Their belief, and their dissonance with the belief of the catholic church, extended all the way back to the exile of Arius after the Council of Nicaea (325), when he was convicted of heresy for contending that "[t]here was a time when he (Jesus) was not," meaning it is possible to imagine a prehistorical moment in which the Father was alone and generated his Son, Jesus. It makes sense that *Quincunque* would feel motivated to push back against this heresy as it reemerged through the Vandal opponents after the sack of Rome in 410.

18. P. Des Maizeaux, *The Life of William Chillingworth* (1725: ed. J. Nichols; London, 1863), 92. Cited in Kelly, *Athanasian Creed*, 124.

19. Ibid., 126.

20. Wilken, "Introducing the Athanasian Creed," 9.

21. Philip Schaff, *History of the Christian Church*, vol. 3, 529. "[T]he whole intention is, not that salvation and perdition depend on the acceptance and rejection of any theological formulary or human conception and exhibition of the truth, but that faith in the revealed truth itself, in the living God, Father, Son, and Spirit, and in Jesus Christ the God-Man and the Savior of the world, is the thing which saves, even where the understanding may be very defective, and that unbelief is the thing which condemns."

Chapter 6: Councils of Constantinople

1. Really "Semi-Arianism." The difference is explained below.

2. Henry Chadwick, "Schism at Antioch: The Council of Constantinople (381)," in *The Church in Ancient Society: From Galilee to Gregory the Great* (Oxford: Oxford Univ. Press, 2001), 9.

3. In Greek, *homoiousian* as opposed to *homoousian*. Considered sellouts by radical Arians, such as the Eunomeans, who maintained that a creature is very different indeed from its creator. See Chadwick, "Schism at Antioch," 2.

4. Jaroslav Pelikan, *The Christian Tradition: A History of the Development of Doctrine*, vol. 1, *The Emergence of the Catholic Tradition (100–600)* (Chicago: Univ. of Chicago Press, 1971), 213.

5. Athanasius, the chief mind behind Nicaea, had made this clear: ibid., 213, and Veli-Matti Karkkainen, ed., *Holy Spirit and Salvation: The Sources of Christian Theology* (Louisville: Westminster John Knox, 2010), 45–47.

6. Karkkainen, *Holy Spirit and Salvation*, 15. The language has been updated for modern readers.

7. Ibid., 17.

8. The idea that the Spirit is a person who speaks to and through believers had been around for some time and can be found (outside the New Testament) as early as Ignatius of Antioch, early second century: "The Spirit made an announcement to me …" (ibid., 6).

9. Ibid.

10. William Bright, *The Canons of the First Four General Councils of Nicaea, Constantinople, Ephesus, and Chalcedon* (Oxford: Clarendon, 1892), 307.

11. Karkkainen, *Holy Spirit and Salvation*, 21.

12. Gregory of Nazianzus, "Fifth Theological Oration (Oration 31)," *http://www .newadvent.org/fathers/310231.htm*, Section XXIX, accessed May 31, 2013.

13. Bright, *Canons of the First Four General Councils*, 310–11.

14. Ibid., 302.

15. On this point, the theologian Basil of Caesarea made much of the fact that Scripture spoke of "by" the Spirit and "with" the Spirit — in other words, the Spirit was the one who did the work. Consider how differently a passage like Ephesians 2:18–22 would read if the Spirit were only a tool: "For through him we both have access in one Spirit to the Father. So then you are no longer strangers and aliens, but you are fellow citizens with the saints and members of the household of God, built on the foundation of the apostles and prophets, Christ Jesus himself being the cornerstone, in whom the whole structure, being joined together, grows into a holy temple in the Lord. In him you also are being built together into a dwelling place for God by the Spirit." See St. Basil the Great, *On the Holy Spirit* (Crestwood, NY: St. Vladimir's Seminary Press, 2001), 22–28.

16. In Greek, from John 15:26. Gregory confessed that he did not know precisely what it means to "proceed"; it is a divine mystery, but the language is from Scripture. However, he suggested that it does mean that the Holy Spirit is eternal, always proceeding from the Father.

17. Emperor Justinian states this goal in the council proceedings themselves: "When, now, the grace of God raised us to the throne, we regarded it as our

chief business to unite the Churches again, and to bring the Synod of Chalcedon, together with the three earlier, to universal acceptance." "Fifth Ecumenical Council: Constantinople II, 553," *http://www.fordham.edu/halsall/basis/const2.asp*, accessed May 31, 2013.

18. G. L. C. Frank, "The Council of Constantinople II as a Model Reconciliation Council," *Theological Studies* 52 (1991): 640.

19. Chadwick, "Schism at Antioch," 5. Origen argued, "What was not assumed is not saved." Since Origen uses the word "assumed" differently than most contemporary readers might be familiar with, I changed it to "taken up."

20. Leo Donald Davis, *The First Seven Ecumenical Councils (325–787): Their History and Theology* (Collegeville, MN: Liturgical Press), 209.

21. Demetrios Bathrellos, *The Byzantine Christ: Person, Nature, and Will in the Christology of Saint Maximus the Confessor* (New York: Oxford Univ. Press, 2004), 55.

22. Frank, "Council of Constantinople II," 645.

23. Along with the Nestorians and Monophysites, who were having their own controversy in the Persian Empire.

24. Bathrellos, *Byzantine Christ*, 70.

25. Ibid., 138.

26. "Sixth Ecumenical Council: Constantinople III (680–681)," *http://www.fordham.edu/halsall/basis/const3.asp*, accessed May 31, 2013.

27. Bathrellos, *Byzantine Christ*, 140.

28. Ibid., 83.

29. "St. Maximus of Constantinople," *http://www.newadvent.org/cathen/10078b.htm*, accessed May 31, 2013.

30. The Maronites, a Syriac Catholic group, are sometimes said to be Monothelite, but that seems to be unfounded: "Maronites," *http://www.newadvent.org/cathen/09683c.htm*, accessed May 31, 2013.

31. Frank, "Council of Constantinople II," 648.

Chapter 7: Councils of Carthage and Orange

1. Henry Chadwick, "Pelagius, Caelestius, and the Roman See in Gaul and North Africa," in *The Church in Ancient Society: From Galilee to Gregory the Great* (Oxford: Oxford Univ. Press, 2001), 3.

2. Ibid., 3.

3. B. R. Rees, *Pelagius: Life and Letters* (Woodbridge: Boydell Press, 1991), 119.

4. Ibid., 168–69.

182 | KNOW THE CREEDS AND COUNCILS

5. J. N. D. Kelly, *Early Christian Doctrines*, rev. ed. (Peabody, MA: Prince Press, 2004), 359.

6. Rees, *Pelagius*, 168. "Impute" is an older legal phrase for "charge" (for example, with a crime). Pelagius is saying that God should not even have to charge us with sin if we are living as we should.

7. See especially Augustine, *Against the Donatists*, Book IV, in which Augustine deals with several questions about the imperfections of the church. Augustine, *Against the Donatists, http://www.newadvent.org/fathers/1408.htm.*

8. Augustine, *The Confessions*, trans. Maria Boulding (New York: New City Press, 2001), 135.

9. Jaroslav Pelikan, *The Christian Tradition: A History of the Development of Doctrine*, vol. 1, *The Emergence of the Catholic Tradition (100–600)* (Chicago: Univ. of Chicago Press, 1971), 299. Augustine therefore sidesteps the drunk-driving analogy from the beginning of the article completely — even though it might *seem* as though humanity were suffering unjustly because of a third party, Augustine would say that everyone was complicit. However, there was a debate at the time as to whether the effects were passed down materially (traducianism) or spiritually (creationism).

10. Ibid., 300. Baptism washes away the guilt and power of original sin. The Catholic Church maintained, however, that *concupiscence*, or the inclination to sin, remained after baptism.

11. "Council of Carthage (A.D. 419)," *http://www.newadvent.org/fathers/3816.htm.* Numbered here as Canon 112, but at the time the fourth of the eight canons passed.

12. Ibid. Numbered here as Canon 113.

13. Chadwick, "Pelagius, Caelestius, and the Roman See," 12. At this point, the Pelagians were "fools, not heretics" in the mind of the church, and only at Ephesus in 431 would they be counted as heretical. Pelikan, *Emergence of the Catholic Tradition*, 316.

14. Chadwick, "Pelagius, Caelestius, and the Roman See," 12.

15. Kelly, *Early Christian Doctrines*, 371.

16. Ibid.

17. The quotation is, "We not only do not believe that any are foreordained to evil by the power of God, but even state with utter abhorrence that if there are those who want to believe so evil a thing, they are anathema."

18. In this respect, the council was not going as far as modern Calvinists. God may call someone to love him, but once the will is freed through baptism, that person can go in any direction he or she chooses. Moreover, since infants were the ones who were usually being baptized, much of the debate was academic, though important to reaffirm the decision at Carthage. For the full text of the

council, see the website of Fordham University: "The Council of Orange," *http://www.fordham.edu/halsall/basis/orange.txt.*

19. David F. Wells, *The Courage to Be Protestant* (Grand Rapids, MI: Eerdmans, 2008), 188.

20. J. Patout Burns, *Theological Anthropology*, Sources of Early Christian Thought (Philadelphia: Fortress, 1981), 1.

Chapter 8: Council of Trent

1. The City of Bologna was on the pope's short list of preferred cities, which meant we might have had the Council of Bologna.

2. Papal infallibility was solemnly defined in 1870 at Vatican I, but it was accepted in the Catholic Church much earlier than that.

3. Robert Bireley, *The Refashioning of Catholicism, 1450–1700* (Washington, DC: Catholic Univ. Press, 1999), 48.

4. H. J. Schroeder, trans., *The Canons and Decrees of the Council of Trent*, (Charlotte: TAN Books and Publishers, 1978), 17.

5. Catholics consider the Apocrypha deuterocanonical books. The term means "belonging to the second canon" and distinguishes these Apocrypha texts both from those considered noncanonical and from those considered protocanonical ("belonging to the first canon").

6. Council of Trent, Session 4: "Decree Concerning the Edition, and the Use, of Sacred Books," *http://history.hanover.edu/texts/trent/ct04.html*, accessed July 25, 2013.

7. It should be noted that when they use this language, they are speaking only of adults. Children experience regeneration through baptism; however, this was not yet discussed at Trent but would be later in the first period.

8. Schroeder, *Canons and Decrees*, 31.

9. "Having, therefore, been thus justified, and made the friends and domestics of God, advancing from virtue to virtue, they are renewed, as the Apostle says, day by day; that is … through the observance of the commandments of God and of the Church, faith co-operating with good works, increase in that justice which they have received through the grace of Christ, and are still further justified, as it is written; He that is just, let him be justified still; and again, Be not afraid to be justified even to death; and also, Do you see that by works a man is justified, and not by faith only. And this increase of justification holy Church begs, when she prays, 'Give unto us, O Lord, increase of faith, hope, and charity.' Session 6, Canon X, "On the Increase of Justification Received," in J. Waterworth, trans., *The Canons and Decrees of the Sacred and Oecumenical Council of Trent* (London: Dolman, 1848), 37.

10. Session 6, Canon VII: "What the Justification of the Impious Is, and What Are the Causes Thereof," in Waterworth *Canons and Decrees*, 35.

11. Ibid.

12. Although it is not relevant for what the council decided, the council was moved temporarily to the papal city of Bologna for part of 1547 because of political strife in the area of Trent. This move is often called a "translation" because the change of location did not mean a new council, but a continuation of the same council.

13. The technical term for this is *ex opere operato* — "from the work done."

14. Joseph F. Kelly, *The Ecumenical Councils of the Catholic Church: A History* (Collegeville, MN: Liturgical Press, 2009), 137. The council "affirmed the presence of Christ under each species, bread and wine, in Holy Communion, asserted the right of the church to limit Communion for the laity to the sacred bread, but left the decision whether to allow Communion under both species or not up to the pope."

15. "For, doubtless, these satisfactory punishments greatly recall from sin, and check as it were with a bridle, and make penitents more cautious and watchful for the future; they are also remedies for the remains of sin, and, by acts of the opposite virtues, they remove the habits acquired by evil living." Bireley, *Refashioning of Catholicism*, 54.

16. Session XIV, 8: "On the Necessity and Fruit of Satisfaction," Waterworth, *Canons and Decrees*, 102–3.

17. Frances Gies, *Marriage and the Family in the Middle Ages* (New York: HarperCollins, 2010), x.

18. Session 24, I, "Decree on the Reformation of Marriage," Waterworth, *Canons and Decrees*, 196.

19. Henry Bettenson and Chris Maunder, eds., *Documents of the Christian Church*, 3rd ed. (Oxford: Oxford Univ. Press, 1999), 277.

20. *http://www.vatican.va/roman_curia/pontifical_councils/chrstuni/documents /rc_pc_chrstuni_doc_31101999_cath-luth-joint-declaration_en.html.*

Chapter 9: Heidelberg Catechism

1. See Richard R. Osmer, "The Case for Catechism," *Christian Century* 114 (1997), 408–12; P. Y. de Jong, "Calvin's Contributions to Christian Education," *Calvin Theological Journal* 2 (1967): 162–201; Philippa Tudor, "Religious Instruction for Children and Adolescents in the Early English Reformation," *Journal of Ecclesiastical History* 35 (1984): 391–413.

2. Calvin and Farel included the catechism in their reform ordinances of 1537. See John Calvin, *Calvin: Theological Treatises* (London: SCM, 1954), 54. Thomas

Cranmer had introduced a catechism to the Church of England in 1549, but it enjoyed relatively little international appeal thanks in large part to the turmoil in England. For a discussion of this development in the Church of England, see I. M. Green, " 'For Children in Yeeres and Children in Understanding': The Emergence of the English Catechism under Elizabeth and the Early Stuarts," *Journal of Ecclesiastical History* 37 (1986): 400.

3. Philip Schaff, *The Creeds of Christendom: With a History and Critical Notes*, 6th ed., vol. 1 (New York: Harper and Brothers, 1919), 535.

4. Zacharias Ursinus, *The Commentary of Dr. Zacharias Ursinus on the Heidelberg Catechism*, trans. G. W. Williard (Cincinnati: T. P. Bucher, 1861), 13–14.

5. Schaff, *Creeds of Christendom*, vol. 1, 541.

6. Ursinus, *Commentary of Dr. Zacharias Ursinus*, 16.

7. The English version of the Heidelberg Catechism mentions the term "election" only in a prooftext for Question 86. Likewise, the term "reprobate" appears only in a prooftext for Question 54.

8. Schaff, *Creeds of Christendom*, vol. 1, 541.

9. The Heidelberg Catechism, Question and Answer 60, *http://www.crcna.org/welcome/beliefs/confessions/heidelberg-catechism*.

10. Schaff, *Creeds of Christendom*, vol. 1, 542.

11. Ibid.

12. Ibid., 551.

Chapter 10: Thirty-nine Articles of Religion

1. Both the terms "Protestant dissenters" and "Calvinists" are used anachronositically. The terms did not take on historical significance and become commonplace until after the Thirty-nine Articles were written. To be precise, one could use the term "Genevan" more appropriately here. While these terms may not have been in use yet at the time we are describing, they are still convenient ways of designating these groups.

2. Contrary to popular opinion, the controversy surrounding Henry VIII's first marriage was over annulment rather than divorce. Divorce would have been steadfastly rejected by all theologians (and, more important, by canon law) of the day. Discussion would not have even begun. The question for Henry's marriage to Catherine of Aragon focused on the legitimacy of a man marrying the widow of his brother. (Catherine of Aragon had previously been married to Henry's older brother, Prince Arthur.)

3. This is in no way meant to say that Henry did not have theological reasons

for his decisions. Contemporary scholarship has revealed a theological side to Henry, though what role that played in his decisions is still up for debate.

4. Mary may have suffered from uterine or ovarian cancer. She also may have succumbed to an influenza outbreak.

5. At the time of the initial revisions, a hope for an English alliance with Lutheran princes on the Continent remained on the horizon. Elizabeth, thus, saw to the deletion of an article (Art. XXIX) that might undermine the potential alliance. This left thirty-eight articles for the Latin edition. When the English edition was prepared in 1571, the hope for alliance with the Lutheran princes had faded. Article XXIX was reinserted, leaving the final (and lasting) version of this confessional document with Thirty-nine Articles.

6. See further, Philip Schaff, *The Creeds of Christendom: With a History and Critical Notes*, 6th ed., vol. 1 (New York: Harper and Brothers, 1919), 622 – 23.

7. Article XIX.

8. Article XXXIV.

9. Article VI.

10. Article XXII.

11. Schaff, *Creeds of Christendom*, vol. 1, 623.

12. Articles IX, X, and XVII, respectively.

13. Article XVII: Of Baptism; Article XXXVII: Of the Power of the Civil Magistrates.

14. For a discussion of this, see Norman Cohn, *The Pursuit of the Millennium: Revolutionary Millenarians and Mystical Anarchists of the Middle Ages* (London: Pimlico, 1993). Also see Crawford Gribben, *The Puritan Millennium* (Milton Keynes: Paternoster, 2008).

15. Articles I and XXXIV. The clearest example of the rationalist sect can be seen in the Polish Brethren, who formed their own movement in 1565 under the teaching and guidance of Fausto Sozzini. This group is often referenced with the name Socinian, from the Anglicized version of Sozzini's name. This group — and others like it — denied the Trinity on rationalist grounds.

16. The Synod of Dort (1619) was the council held in modern-day Netherlands, which condemned the theology of the Remonstrants (followers of Jacob Arminius) and established the so-called five points of Calvinism. The English representatives were not as extreme in their view of the doctrine of predestination as many of the participants at Dort, but they were able to assent to the final decrees while holding to the official teaching of the Thirty-nine Articles.

17. John Henry Newman converted from Anglicanism to Roman Catholicism, eventually being named a Cardinal in 1879.

18. Article XVII.

Chapter 11: Westminster Confession of Faith

1. Ordinance for the Assembly of Divines, in John Rushworth, *Mr. Rushworth's Historical Collections Abridg'd and Improv'd* (6 vols; London: s.n., 1706–8), V:123.

2. Specifically, the Solemn League and Covenant, the document that aligned the English Parliament and Scotland, expressly noted the desire to have "nearest conjunction and uniformity in religion, Confession of Faith, Form of Church Government, Directory for Worship and Catechising." To meet this task, the assembly began work on the production of the Confession of Faith, the Larger and Shorter Catechisms, the Directory of Public Worship, and an explanation of acceptable church polity. The Confession of Faith and the two catechisms were published together in 1649, complete with prooftexts. Prior to this, the documents had been printed separately, mainly for perusal of Parliament and members of the assembly.

3. The final ordinance that summoned the Westminster Assembly of Divines called for this synod to consider "such matters and things, touching and concerning the Liturgy, discipline, and government of the Church of England, or the vindicating and clearing of the doctrine of the same from all false aspersions and misconstructions, as shall be proposed to them by both or either of the said Houses of Parliament, and no other." Ordinance for the Assembly of Divines (19 Car. I c. 6), in Rushworth, *Mr. Rushworth's Historical Collections*, V:123.

4. The Confession of Faith and the two catechisms were published together in 1649, complete with prooftexts. Prior to this, the documents had been printed separately, mainly for perusal of Parliament and members of the assembly.

5. Chapter 9, Paragraph 3.

6. Chapter 3, Paragraph 3.

7. Chapter 11, Paragraph 4.

8. Chapter 10, Paragraph 1.

9. Chapter 17, Paragraph 1.

10. Westminster Confession and Catechisms, Article 3.iii.

11. Westminster Confession and Catechisms, Article 9.

12. Westminster Confession and Catechisms, Article 15.

13. A synod is a council or an assembly of church officials or churches.

14. John Frame, "Westminster Confession of Faith," in *Evangelical Dictionary of Theology*, ed. Walter Elwell (Grand Rapids, MI: Baker, 1984), 1168–69.

15. Ibid. Additionally, this confession led directly to the development of two other confessions — the Savoy Declaration for the Independents and the Second

London Confession for the Particular Baptists — increasing the influence of the WCF exponentially.

16. Justification is being declared righteous and forgiven of sins because of the work of Christ. Sanctification is God freeing sinners in Christ Jesus from slavery to sin so that they may live for God by faith with a love for God in heart and life. Glorification is the receiving of perfection by the elect before entering into the kingdom of heaven and the receiving of the resurrection bodies by the elect.

17. The prooftexts provided with the confession also can be seen as demonstrating this point. However, one should note that the divines did not originally include these prooftexts. They were added only at the request of Parliament after the entire confession had been approved.

18. This term does not normally have a specific referent, alternatively identifying all predestinarian Reformed theology, only the theology stemming from the Synod of Dort, or any theology focused on a covenant of grace.

19. But maybe we should. A recent case in Britain ruled that since some Christians work on Sundays, it is not a religious right to take the day off: "Christians and Working on Sundays: What the Tribunal Really Said," *http://www.guardian .co.uk/law/2013/jan/10/employment-tribunal-christians-working-sundays*, accessed July 26, 2013.

Chapter 12: Second Vatican Council

1. John W. O'Malley, *What Happened at Vatican II* (Cambridge: Belknap Press, 2008), 89–90.

2. Joseph F. Kelly, *The Ecumenical Councils of the Catholic Church: A History* (Collegeville, MN: Liturgical Press, 2009), 179.

3. Ibid., 182.

4. O'Malley, *What Happened at Vatican II*, 40.

5. Quoted in ibid., 39.

6. Richard R. Gaillardetz and Catherine E. Clifford, *Keys to the Council: Unlocking the Teaching of Vatican II* (Collegeville, MN: Liturgical Press, 2012), 18.

7. *Dei Verbum*, 3: *http://www.vatican.va/archive/hist_councils/ii_vatican_council/ documents/vat-ii_const_19651118_dei-verbum_en.html*, accessed July 16, 2013.

8. Henry Bettenson and Chris Maunder, eds., *Documents of the Christian Church*, 3rd ed. (Oxford: Oxford Univ. Press, 1999), 362.

9. Ibid., 364.

Chapter 13: Modern Confessions: Lausanne Covenant and Chicago Statement on Biblical Inerrancy

1. I use the term "council" for the gatherings that led to the Chicago Statement on Biblical Inerrancy and the Lausanne Covenant. The Chicago statement was drafted by members of the International Council on Biblical Inerrancy. The Lausanne Movement hosts global congresses and regional consultations. So in this sense "council" is a generic term for a gathering, not to be confused with an ecumenical council discussed previously in this book.

2. "Muratorian Fragment," *http://www.earlychristianwritings.com/muratorian .html*, accessed July 17, 2013.

3. Ibid.

4. J. N. D. Kelly, *Early Christian Doctrines*, rev. ed. (Peabody, MA: Prince Press, 2004), 61.

5. Reductionism is the belief that the simplest explanation is the best. For instance, a reductionist might argue that the urge for a mother to protect her child is just a biological response, rather than a matter of love or genuine self-sacrifice. Since biology provides an adequate explanation of why the mother acts, the reductionist will not consider love as a motive unless it becomes very clear that the simplest theory does not make the best use of the evidence.

6. In the early twentieth century, the fundamentalists were those who were concerned with preserving orthodox tenets. The extreme version is only one subset.

7. Millard Erickson, *Christian Theology*, 3rd ed. (Grand Rapids, MI: Baker, 2013), 246.

8. "(1) God, who is Himself Truth and speaks truth only, has inspired Holy Scripture in order thereby to reveal Himself to lost mankind through Jesus Christ as Creator and Lord, Redeemer and Judge. Holy Scripture is God's witness to Himself.

   "(2) Holy Scripture, being God's own Word, written by men prepared and superintended by His Spirit, is of infallible divine authority in all matters upon which it touches: it is to be believed, as God's instruction, in all that it affirms: obeyed, as God's command, in all that it requires; embraced, as God's pledge, in all that it promises.

   "(3) The Holy Spirit, Scripture's divine Author, both authenticates it to us by His inward witness and opens our minds to understand its meaning.

   "(4) Being wholly and verbally God-given, Scripture is without error or fault in all its teaching, no less in what it states about God's acts in creation, about the events of world history, and about its own literary origins under God, than in its witness to God's saving grace in individual lives.

   "(5) The authority of Scripture is inescapably impaired if this total divine inerrancy is in any way limited or disregarded, or made relative to a view of truth contrary to the Bible's own; and such lapses bring serious loss to both the individual and the Church."

9. *http://www.bible-researcher.com/chicago1.html.*

10. "The Chicago Statement on Biblical Inerrancy: Exposition C," *http://www.spurgeon.org/~phil/creeds/chicago.htm*, accessed July 17, 2013.

11. "The Chicago Statement on Biblical Inerrancy: Exposition E," *http://www.spurgeon.org/~phil/creeds/chicago.htm*, accessed July 17, 2013.

12. *http://www.bible-researcher.com/chicago1.html.*

13. Because there are a large number of variations in the New Testament manuscripts, some argue that the words of the New Testament are unreliable. But the vast number of New Testament manuscripts actually enables us to figure out what the originals said with a great deal of certainty. As Mark Roberts puts it, "having many manuscripts actually increases the likelihood of our getting back to the original text." Mark D. Roberts, *Can We Trust the Gospels? Investigating the Reliability of Matthew, Mark, Luke, and John* (Wheaton, IL: Crossway, 2007). Scholars are able to compare the various manuscripts containing the same passages of Scripture and determine, on the basis of internal and external evidence, which of the manuscripts most likely gets the original wording right. For more on this topic see, "Why You Can Trust Your Bible," *http://justinholcomb.com/2013/08/16/why-you-can-trust-your-bible/.*

14. John Stott, "Introduction to Covenant," *http://www.lausanne.org/docs/lau1docs/0002.pdf.*

15. Ibid.

16. Georges-Andre Chevallaz, "Opening Greetings," available at *http://www.lausanne.org/docs/lau1docs/0010.pdf*, accessed May 24, 2013.

17. "We also affirm the power of God's word to accomplish his purpose of salvation. The message of the Bible is addressed to all men and women. For God's revelation in Christ and in Scripture is unchangeable. Through it the Holy Spirit still speaks today. He illumines the minds of God's people in every culture to perceive its truth freshly through their own eyes and thus discloses to the whole Church ever more of the many-colored wisdom of God." Lausanne Covenant 2. See also Susuma Uda, "Biblical Authority and Evangelism," *http://www.lausanne.org/docs/lau1docs/0079.pdf*, accessed June 11, 2013. In this emphasis Lausanne is at home in the Reformation tradition. The Westminster Confession of Faith declares, for instance, that "[t]he supreme judge by which all controversies of religion are to be determined, and all decrees of councils, opinions of ancient writers, doctrines of men, and private spirits, are to be examined, and in whose sentence we are to rest, can be no other but the Holy Spirit speaking in the Scripture" (WCF 1.10). See also Richard Muller, *Post-Reformation Reformed Dogmatics*, vol. 2, *Holy Scripture* (Grand Rapids, MI: Baker Academic, 2002).

It is important to note that neither the Manila Manifesto nor the Capetown Commitment include this emphasis as clearly.

18. Lausanne Covenant 9; Manila Manifesto 6, *http://www.lausanne.org/en/documents /manila-manifesto.html*, accessed June 11, 2013; The Capetown Commitment IID1, *http://www.lausanne.org/en/documents/ctcommitment.html*, accessed June 11, 2013.

19. Lausanne Covenant 4, *http://www.lausanne.org/en/documents/lausanne-covenant.html*, accessed June 3, 2013.

20. Lausanne Covenant 4. See also, Gottfried Osei-Mensah, "The Holy Spirit in World Evangelization," *http://www.lausanne.org/docs/lau1docs/0259.pdf*, accessed June 11, 2013. This point is accented by Manila Manifesto 5: "The Scriptures declare that God himself is the chief evangelist. For the Spirit of God is the Spirit of truth, love, holiness and power, and evangelism is impossible without him. It is he who anoints the messenger, confirms the word, prepares the hearer, convicts the sinful, enlightens the blind, gives life to the dead, enables us to repent and believe, unites us to the Body of Christ, assures us that we are God's children, leads us into Christlike character and service, and sends us out in our turn to be Christ's witnesses. In all this the Holy Spirit's main preoccupation is to glorify Jesus Christ by showing him to us and forming him in us." See also Capetown Commitment I1. In particular, Lausanne is incompatible with the "New Measures" evangelism associated with Charles Finney and D. L. Moody. See, for example, George Marsden, *Fundamentalism and American Culture*; Charles Hambrick-Stowe, *Charles Finney and the Spirit of American Evangelicalism*; Lyle Dorsett, *A Passion for Souls: The Life of D. L. Moody*. For a contemporary nineteenth-century critique of the New Measures, see J. W. Nevin, *The Anxious Bench* (1843).

21. Lausanne Covenant 12. See Bruno Herm, "Prayer in Evangelization," *http:// www.lausanne.org/docs/lau1docs/*, accessed June 11, 2013.

22. The covenant, for instance, calls world leaders to act in accordance with the Universal Declaration of Human Rights of the United Nations. Lausanne Covenant 13.

23. Lausanne Covenant 11. See Henri Blocher, "The Nature of Biblical Unity," *http://www.lausanne.org/docs/lau1docs/0380.pdf*, accessed June 11, 2013.

24. Lausanne Covenant 14.

25. For example, 9: "We cannot hope to attain this goal without sacrifice. All of us are shocked by the poverty of millions and disturbed by the injustices which cause it. Those of us who live in affluent circumstances accept our duty to develop a simple life-style in order to contribute more generously to both relief and evangelism." See also "An Evangelical Commitment to a Simple Life-style," Lausanne Occasional Papers 20, Paragraph 5: "We intend to reexamine our

income and expenditure, in order to manage on less and give away more. We lay down no rules or regulations, for either ourselves or others. Yet we resolve to renounce waste and oppose extravagance in personal living, clothing and housing, travel and church buildings. We also accept the distinction between necessities and luxuries, creative hobbies and empty status symbols, modesty and vanity, occasional celebrations and normal routine, and between the service of God and slavery to fashion." Available at *www.lausanne.org/en/documents /lops/77-lop–20.html*, accessed June 11, 2013.

26. The literary productions of the Lausanne Movement can be found at *www .lausanne.org*.

27. Cf. John Webster, "Confession and Confessions," in *Confessing God: Essays in Christian Dogmatics II* (London: T&T Clark, 2005), 71.

28. Ibid.

29. Ibid.

30. Ibid.

31. I used this term broadly to include creeds, confessions, and catechisms.

32. Webster, "Confession and Confessions," 69.

33. Ibid.

34. Ibid.

35. C. S. Lewis, "Introduction," in St. Athanasius, *De Incarnatione Verbi Dei* (Crestwood, NY: St. Vladimir's Seminary Press, 1944, 1993), 4–5.